Politics of the Everyday

T0353540

DESIGNING IN DARK TIMES

The series 'Designing in Dark Times' pushes at the boundaries of contemporary design thinking, engaging with the world's current and pressing social, economic and environmental crises.

Exploring the interaction of design with social understanding and presenting both modes of thought (models, concepts, arguments) and courses of action (scenarios, strategies, proposals, works), titles engage polemically with the opportunities now presented to rethink what acting and designing could be.

FORTHCOMING TITLES IN THE SERIES

Politics of the Everyday

Ezio Manzini

Translated from the Italian by
Rachel Anne Coad

BLOOMSBURY VISUAL ARTS
LONDON • NEW YORK • OXFORD • NEW DELHI • SYDNEY

BLOOMSBURY VISUAL ARTS
Bloomsbury Publishing Plc
50 Bedford Square, London, WC1B 3DP, UK
1385 Broadway, New York, NY 10018, USA

BLOOMSBURY, BLOOMSBURY VISUAL ARTS and the Diana logo are
trademarks of Bloomsbury Publishing Plc

First published in Great Britain 2019
Paperback reprinted 2022

Copyright © Ezio Manzini, 2019
Translation: © Rachel Anne Coad

A catalogue record for this book is available from the British Library.

A catalog record for this book is available from the Library of Congress.

ISBN: HB: 978-1-3500-5365-6
       PB: 978-1-3500-5364-9
       ePub: 978-1-3500-5366-3
       ePDF: 978-1-3500-5367-0

Typeset by Integra Software Services Pvt. Ltd.

To find out more about our authors and books visit www.bloomsbury.com
and sign up for our newsletter.

CONTENTS

FOREWORD

Designing in Dark Times/ The Urgency of the Possible

Responding to the current and wide-ranging systemic, social, economic, political, and environmental challenges we face, the aim of this new series—of which Ezio Manzini's *The Politics of the Everyday* is the opening contribution—is to bring together a series of short, polemical texts that address these crises and their inherent possibilities. Understanding that the old division between the theoretical focus of the sciences and the practical stance integral to designing, making, and shaping the world is dissolving, *Designing in Dark Times* explores new ways of acting and knowing concerning the artificial. Identified by a refusal of resignation to what-is and by the equal necessity and urgency of developing new models of the possible and Presenting both modes of thought (models, concepts, arguments) and courses of action (scenarios, strategies, proposals, works)—at all levels from the local and the micro (the situation) to the global and the macro (the universal)—the aim is to push the boundaries of both design and thought, to make each more capable of opening genuine possibilities for thinking and acting otherwise and thus of better facing, and facing down, the myriad failures of the present. Re-thinking the relation between justice and making, and between material human needs and the means and modes of how these can be realized, *Designing in Dark Times* is conceived as a contribution to the wider necessities of dealing with a vulnerable precarious world, of establishing project not profit as the basis of action, and of building the bases for wide-ranging emancipatory politics. As the world descends into crisis, these books seek to offer, in small ways, a counter view. Against the instrumental they use the fact that design is *also* a means of articulating hitherto unforeseen possibilities—for subjects as much as for the world—to show how at base it offers irreplaceable capabilities for thinking and acting well in the artificial. In so doing, they point us toward ways of reversing some of negative and destructive tendencies threatening to engulf the world.

Clive Dilnot, for the editorial group of *Designing in Dark Times*, March 2018

PREFACE

You are here: A point of view and action on the world

1. Many years ago, I was struck by a picture showing a mass of stars and galaxies with an arrow indicating a white dot and the words "You are here." At the time this picture said something important to me, but I was still a child and I did not really understand. Now I believe I understand it a little better: we human beings are somewhere in a great universe, in its enormous complexity. Yet on the other hand we are here, and from where we stand, from that tiny spot of universe in which we happen to be, we act, we think, and we transform the things around us: we live.

Starting from us, and from where we are, is not therefore an expression of irreducible anthropocentrism. On the contrary, it is an acknowledgment of a limit: humbly recognizing that whatever we think and do, we cannot but think it and do it from the point where we find ourselves.

This point of view and action on the world, for me, is the *hyperlocal*. In this context, the prefix "hyper" has two meanings: it is obviously something very local, but it is also, and today more than ever, a boundless local from which we can see and act far away, yet always and only from the point where we stand.

In this book, I assume this viewpoint in order to discuss the nature and political sense of our life projects, starting from their everyday existence. In order to do this, we must recognize the complexity of the world and the relativity of what we can think, trying to navigate the first and accept the second with the limits it imposes.

In this spirit, each of the four chapters that make up the book starts with an observation of situations located within 20 kilometers from where I live. There is nothing really special about any of them; they are moments of life caught in their normality and in their singularity. However, since any other situation I might have chosen to describe would have been equally normal and unique, I thought it would be worth starting with these personal cases. At least I know them better.

2. The book was born from my experience as a designer in the field of social innovation and seeks to make a contribution to the diffusion of a critical, collaborative design capability. It is not a sociology book or a book of political science; neither is it a manual of everyday-life design. It is, or at least it would like to be, a book of design culture, whose potential readership includes everyone who is involved in design activities—and so, effectively, anybody.

I have chosen as my interlocutor a person whom I imagine to be curious and intelligent but not necessarily an expert. This has had an effect on the way I have written the bibliographic references and the notes: I have reduced the former to a minimum and have used the notes to signal anything and anyone who has particularly influenced me in the writing of what I have written.

1

Light Communities: Social Forms in a Fluid World

Near the village where I live, there is an age-old holm oak tree (*quercus ilex*) standing in an enticing clearing amid vineyards and woodlands. One summer evening, toward sunset, a mixed medley of people are standing around it under its huge arching boughs, which reach down almost to the ground creating a magnificent leafy chamber. At the center, near its trunk, there is a group of actors reciting passages from the *Odyssey*, accompanied by three musicians playing contemporary music. Later on, there will be wine and food. The sun is setting. A moment of shared happiness. Even though …

Even though we all know that elsewhere, at that precise moment, people are fleeing and others are being shot at by snipers, others are dying of hunger. For others, there are no trees to gather around. Others, many others, are not in such dramatic conditions, but just the same they have no possibility of living a moment like this—because they have no such tree, or they are unable to recognize it. Why is it then that here all this (still) exists?

What I would like to talk about is how such special moments come to be: moments when everyone is happy just because they feel that everyone around them is happy too, happy with themselves and happy with the world. It seems to me that this condition of shared happiness does not mean indifference or unawareness of the life of others who are less fortunate. It does not cancel out that horror at the indifference, egoism, and violence proliferating in the world. Instead, with its simple, delicate existence it indicates that things could also be different from what is so often implied—different from the view that happiness is the result of competitive success and the benefits that may derive from it. That circle of people around a tree, listening to words and music and eating together, says that another scenario is possible, and this may point to a direction for action. Am I exaggerating? Am I giving too much responsibility to a group of people around a tree? Maybe I am, but I believe that we should be able to recognize there a seed of a new civilization and an image of a possible future, one that we can see emerging in places and moments like this.

So, taking this example further, who are these people? Why are they there? How do they come to be there? The people around the holm oak are a variegated piece of the world: some have been living in the area for generations, others have chosen to live there, and still others represent the new nomads—tourists or migrants as may be. Each of them has a network of relationships that includes some of those present, but above all it connects them with other people, local or otherwise, scattered around the physical and the digital world. At this moment and in this place, these different networks will intertwine with each other producing a denser fabric of people, places, and things. They express and produce a community: a new contemporary form of community that, unlike the communities of the past, has not been handed down to them. This is a community that exists by choice, one that has been consciously or unconsciously designed and built.

When I talk about community in this book, I am referring to this type of community: voluntary, light, open communities, in which the individuality of each member is balanced with the desire to do something together; fluid communities, without which there is only the solitude of connected individuality or a reactionary attempt to reproduce the closed identitarian communities of the past, which, even supposing they were once so appealing, were certainly part of a past that cannot return.

So why are those people there and not shut in their houses? We have already given the immediate answer: they are there because they recognize the value of a moment of shared happiness and see it as a shared good. In trying to unravel the meaning of this phrase, we find various threads: interest for the theatrical and musical performance and interest for the food and wine; the pleasure of meeting up with old friends or of meeting new people; the beauty of the place; the magic of an ancient tree. The reasons are therefore different in substance and nature. They are a mixture of something that can be produced and bought or given and something that nobody can produce individually but which is created together, with time: the beauty of that tree in the clearing and the ability to recognize it; the rediscovery of a shared root in the extracts from the *Odyssey*, which almost everybody here has studied or at least heard at some point in their lives; and the sense of trust and empathy that the moment produces. Shared happiness is based on the recognition of these commons.

How could all this come about? Obviously, everything I have described is not a natural phenomenon; it exists because someone made it to happen. It has always been so. In this very place, if we go back in time, we can find many similar situations: many different circles of people around a tree or a fire or someone playing an instrument or reciting in ottava rima. Of course, there was food and wine. But here the analogy with our circle of people around the holm oak ends. The people who were there in those groups in times past had not really chosen to be there. More often than not, in past communities, things were that way because they had always been so. The place, the food, the music, and the theater were there because they had always been there (or at least, that was how it seemed), and the people were there because that was "the done thing." This system of traditions, and the conventional way of thinking and doing things that this entailed, is no longer with us—or is barely so. It certainly does not lie behind the scene I have described. Everyone could have been elsewhere. No one has made anyone else come. Things are like this because everyone, in different roles, has done their part.

Before abandoning this initial image, I would like to point out how fragile the community is that we see there and thus the sense of shared happiness it produces. It would only need the landowner to decide he no longer wants other people on his property and things would fall apart. The local government, faced with budget cuts, might withdraw the support it still offers today with such foresight. The organizers might decide, for shortsighted economic reasons, to promote the event only with tourists and thus reduce the presence of the very group that provides the necessary continuity—the local residents. Even an increase in the number of ill-mannered people unable to visit a place without scattering it with refuse and fag ends would be fatal. The list of possible pejorative agents could go on, and here we need this reminder to make it clear that when we have an experience like this, we must be well aware that we are in the midst of something that is as precious as it is fragile. We must nurture it, with a care that comes from everybody interested. But who constitutes this "everybody" I am talking about? Why am I calling them a community and not simply a temporary aggregation of individuals?

Fluidity

If the world becomes fluid. The world seems to be losing solidity:[1] its organizations are becoming malleable and the life-

---

[1] I made this statement for the first time about thirty years ago when, like many others at the time, I "discovered complexity." Reading Edgar Morin was important for me in this respect, but much was also contributed by the thinking of Michel Serres. I will come back to these authors later, for now I will just say that they taught me to look at the fluid world not only as a risk but also as an opportunity for new possibilities: a way of seeing things that I think is still valid despite the many changes that have taken place since then. Indeed, it constitutes the background not only of the first chapter but of the entire book. Edgar Morin, *La Méthode 1. La Nature de la Nature* (Paris: Seuil, 1977); Michel Serres, *La naissance de la physique dans le texte de Lucrèce: fleuves et turbulences* (Paris: Éditions de Minuit, 1977).

forms taking place in it are becoming fluid; every project tends to be flexible and every choice reversible—or at least that is what we think.

The characteristics of this (almost) fluid world have grown out of the (almost) solid ones of the past. The agricultural and industrial societies of past centuries were highly viscous systems, so, in practice, they were solid (or so it was thought): solid were the social and production organizations, solid the communities and personal ties, solid the ideas of well-being (which were in turn mainly based on the solidity of things: land, home, goods possessed and consumed). This solidity was to a large extent a consequence of the difficulty in penetrating space (which made people reluctant to move things and people) and of the limits in transmitting information (restricting the spread of ideas and the spatial distribution of organizations). All this in turn had created a second stability factor: the durability of social conventions and cultural traditions and thus resistance to organizational transformation.

The whole panorama has changed in recent times: connectivity has dissolved organizations as heat melts solid materials. Social conventions have slackened their grip, as have the communities of the past. Strong, long-lasting ties are evaporating, and light, variable social networks are appearing. These changes produce effects that worry many, including this writer: this fluid world colonized by neoliberal ideas and a neoliberal economy is becoming a world of connected solitude, of precarious jobs and of extreme inequalities. It lacks visions of the future. This is the world of liquid modernity, so masterfully represented by Zygmunt Bauman.[2]

For my part, I share the worries of Bauman and of those who, like him, describe the tragedy of the fluid world as it

---

[2] Zygmunt Bauman was a Polish sociologist and philosopher who best summed up the most characterizing aspect of contemporary society in his expression "liquid modernity." Zygmunt Bauman, *Liquid Modernity* (Cambridge, UK: Polity, 2000); Zygmunt Bauman, *Wasted Lives. Modernity and Its Outcasts* (Oxford: Blackwell Publishing, 2004).

appears today. However, I would like to separate the fluid nature of contemporary reality from the problems it generates and hypothesize that the fluid world could be better than what we are living in today. Maybe it could even be better than the solid world of the past. After all, it is precisely the solid world of the past or, to be more exact, the culture that made us see it as solid that has led us to the environmental and social disaster we find ourselves in. Maybe the metaphor of a fluid world can help us to see how we can live there in a way that is lighter and more adaptable to the mobility of everything around us.

Acknowledging the fluidity of things is nothing new in the history of Western culture. As Michel Serres wrote years ago,[3] throughout the history of Western philosophy, there have been two parallel ways of describing the world: one that saw it as a solid world, made of stable things, and the other that interpreted it as a fluid world, made of moving particles. So, for Serres, adopting an interpretive model means *simply* going back to Democritus and Lucretius and the world of Venus against that of Mars. However, science too takes us in the same direction. Today we know that nature and human beings and their interactions are complex entities and that their complexity can be described better by referring to the fluid forms of living systems, rather than the solid ones of minerals. Thus, looking at the world and acknowledging its fluidity may be a first step toward abandoning the mechanistic (and therefore ineffective) interpretative models of the past and at last really coming to terms with its complexity. This also means seeing not only problems when grappling with the practical complexities of everyday life but also new and previously unconceivable possibilities.[4]

---

[3] Michel Serres is a French writer and philosopher. Here, I'm referring in particular to his book: Serres, *La naissance de la physique dans le texte de Lucrèce*.

[4] There are many roads that lead to the discovery of complexity. In my case I arrived thirty years ago, through the thoughts of Edgar Morin. Morin is a French philosopher and sociologist, who was among the first to take the

The fluid world model can easily be adapted to describe how things are going today, in general and for social forms in particular, both for describing the problems that come up and for finding solutions to them. For now, let's ask ourselves this simple question: How are these forms generated and how are they kept alive?

For the solid world, the answer may have seemed obvious: the forms were created by acting on materials (in a physical or metaphorical way). Then they lasted because, being solid, they had a natural propensity to do so, unless something happened. In other words, things could be produced and once they had been produced, if nothing else happened, they were destined to last. Obviously it was not like that, or at least not precisely like that, but for a long time this was the dominant way of seeing things. In a world where changes happened slowly, it enabled reality to be interpreted with an adequate degree of precision.

What changes if we refer to the fluid world? Experience tells us that in a fluid world also forms are created, like a whirlpool or the laminar structure of a fluid-flow. This happens when many particles are induced by their surroundings to move in an orderly way. When this happens, the form produces itself and remains as long as the surrounding conditions that generated it remain unchanged.

This way of looking at things leads us also to see the result of our actions as an interweave of fluid forms, the existence of which is made possible and probable by acting on their environment and that will last as long as these conditions remain. In other words, in a fluid world, for social forms to emerge they require favorable conditions to be created, which then need to be taken care of.

"Creating favorable conditions" and "taking care" are two activities that assume a fundamental role when we adopt this

---

question of the crisis of the mechanistic model from the field of science to that of philosophy and its implications for people's lives. Morin, *La Méthode 1. La Nature de la Nature.*

interpretive model, one that characterizes human activity. In the solid world, people were led to imagine themselves, or imagine others, as powerful individuals able to leave an indelible mark: demiurges able to impact directly on the world, changing it forever. By contrast, the fluid world talks about collective action as the only possibility for building favorable environments. It tells us about the importance of attention and of listening to things in the long term, about care for their upkeep. In short, it tells us the importance of caring.

Transformative social innovation. The fluid world as we know it today is characterized by the diffusion, and now by the crisis, of neoliberal economic models, ideas, and political practices.[5] It is not the intention of this book to go into their nature and tragic consequences. However, their pervasiveness is such that it is not possible to tackle the issues we are dealing with here without taking it into account or, in other words, without considering that by colonizing technological innovation it has concentrated enormous quantities of power and wealth into just a few hands, creating unemployment, underemployment, marginalization, and, as a reaction, the antidemocratic involution that we are seeing in various parts of the world. Furthermore, by trying to relegate every aspect of life to the realm of competition and economic efficiency, it is exasperating the processes of social disaggregation, desertification of all that is public and relational, and the commercialization of common goods.

---

[5] Criticism of neoliberalism has produced endless literature. I will quote Joseph Stiglitz, Noam Chomsky, and David Harvey as examples—three authors who have been important to me in different ways. They come from very different backgrounds and hold very different political positions but in the polyphony of their voices, I think, they give consistency and depth to the criticism. Among their many books, see Joseph Stiglitz, *The Great Divide. Unequal Societies and What We Can Do about Them* (New York: W. W. Norton & Company, 2015); Noam Chomsky, *Who Rules the World* (Henry Holt and Company, 2016); David Harvey, *A Brief History of Neoliberalism* (Oxford, UK: Oxford University Press, 2017).

Nevertheless, pervasive as the neoliberal ways of thinking and behaving are, they do not occupy the entire stage. A careful scrutiny of contemporary reality shows us a composite and dynamic social landscape, in which other ways of thinking and acting exist. They are the result of the initiative of creative, enterprising people who, when faced with a problem or an opportunity, come up with new solutions and put them into practice. These are solutions endowed with values that are individual and social at the same time, ranging from mutual-help groups to care communities or from small-scale production to the regeneration of urban commons. Such initiatives tend to (re)connect people, (re)connect people with the places where they live, and regenerate mutual trust and ability to dialogue— and by so doing they create new communities.

Produced at first by small groups of enthusiasts, with time these activities have grown, evolved, and met with institutional acknowledgment, to the point where they represent significant countertrends that can be found in all ambits of everyday life: collaborative social services, various forms of distributed and open production, collaborative welfare, food networks based on a new relationship between producers and consumers, and proposals for cities seen as commons. A common characteristic in all these examples is that the people involved have broken with the individualism proposed by the dominant culture and have decided to collaborate in order to achieve results, together, that have value for each of them and for everybody or, in other words, for each of the participants and for society as a whole.

All these activities that start from small group initiatives, yet may manage to impact on the institutions and on policy even at a large scale, constitute what I shall refer to from now on as *social innovation*: a term that has been widely used over the last few years, with various meanings.[6] For me it means

---

[6] The conceptualization and diffusion of the social innovation phenomenon, as it appeared at the start of this century, have been largely driven by English researchers from the Young Foundation and Nesta. Therefore, I think it is both

the following: a change in the socio-technical system, the nature and results of which *also* have social value, with the double connotation of solution to social problems and of (re) generation of physical and social commons.

To achieve these results, the systemic change produced has to be radical. This entails redefining the meaning system in which questions are put and solutions found and, in so doing, redefining relationships between the actors, including the power relations that characterize them.

Finally, but for me, it is precisely this that makes this social innovation so interesting: because it is based on collaboration and because it regenerates the commons, social innovation is critical of the dominant ideas and practices and what it proposes could constitute concrete steps toward social and environmental sustainability.

Having said this, we must make it clear that this social innovation, *transformative social innovation*,[7] is a subset of social innovation as a whole. Indeed, there are innovations that go in different directions from the one I am indicating: ones that are not radical in character, but limit themselves to proposing incremental modifications, or that go in a direction that is completely opposite to that of environmental and social sustainability. Thus, it must be understood that when I write "social innovation" in this book, the expression should be read

---

right and useful here to give their best-considered definition: "We define social innovations as new ideas (products, services and models) that simultaneously meet social needs (more effectively than alternatives) and create new social relationships or collaborations. In other words they are innovations that are both good for society and enhance society's capacity to act." In Robin Murray, Julie Caulier Grice, and Geoff Mulgan, *Open Book of Social Innovation* (London: Nesta & the Young Foundation, 2010).

[7] The expression "transformative social innovation" was introduced in the ambits of the European research project Transit, which ended in 2017. The task was to investigate "transformative social network initiatives and networks in an attempt to understand the process of societal transformation" (in Transit, *Doing Things Differently*. Transit Brief #1, 2017, http://www. transitsocialinnovation.eu).

as an abbreviation for social innovation that transforms the existent by taking steps toward sustainability.

Local discontinuity in the transition. After almost half a century of research and experimentation concerning the transition toward sustainability, we now know for certain that it requires a radical change in the cultural and socio-technical system. The size and profundity of this change will not be unlike that seen in the evolution of feudal society into what is generally called the modern, industrial society. Only the difference today, given our global interconnection, will probably be that it will not take so long and that right from the start it will involve the entire planet.[8]

Today, we also know that large-scale systemic changes occur when there is an accumulation of small-scale radical changes. However, incremental changes do not prepare systemic changes and so they are not steps toward sustainability. For example, buying a car with an engine that reduces carbon emissions into the atmosphere may certainly contribute to a local improvement in air quality, and this is positive, but it does not affect the transport system, which continues to be based on the individual car mobility that is the origin of its intrinsic unsustainability. On the other hand, leaving the private car and going by bike, or on foot, or organizing a car pooling activity modifies the local system and therefore contributes to creating conditions for a major systemic change. The same is true for people who stop buying fruit and vegetables from the large-scale retail trade and join an ethical purchasing group or other forms of direct relationship with local producers. These are all cases of transformative social innovation, which produces a discontinuity, that is, a systemic change, on a local scale.

---

[8] On this subject too the literature is unlimited. For the fundamental questions, it is useful to read the works of the Stockholm Resilience Centre on the question of the Anthropocene and its limits (http://www.stockholmresilience. org/research/research-news/2017-02-16-wef-2017-beyond-the-anthropocene. html). Thomas Hylland Eriksen, *Overheating: An Anthropology of Accelerated Change* (London: Pluto Press, 2016).

These examples tell us something important, which needs highlighting: the transition toward sustainability entails a huge and highly complex change. Because of this, it cannot be driven from the control tower; it has to begin from within, from changes inside its local subsets—from something local that could and indeed should *also* be the micro-local of everyday choices. These are choices that anyone can make, if they want to: to change your diet and stop eating meat you just have to decide, there is no need to ask anyone; it is the same to go by bike instead of by car (providing you are able to ride a bike). To start some form of collaborative housing you only need to come to an agreement with a group of neighbors. I am not suggesting that this is easy. Each of these choices requires a redefinition of the meaning of things and the priorities we give them. I am just trying to say that in our daily lives systemic change is not something to put off until the future. It can and must be done now, sometimes by individual choice, more often by collaborative decisions. It is this immediate feasibility of taking concerted steps toward sustainability that is the most important message social innovation is giving us.

However, we should clarify the meaning of the adjective "local" in this context. It does not necessarily refer to small-scale events of the kind I have mentioned so far. It means that the system that changes is a part—a local dimension—of a wider system whereby just as a person switching from a car to a bike generates a local discontinuity (presuming cycling was not already a consolidated habit in the area), so does a city when it decides to modify its traffic circulation against the prevailing ideas and practice in the region, introducing cycle lanes and other alternative forms of mobility. Furthermore, as we can surmise from the previous examples, what may be a discontinuity in one place may well not be in another: cycling in Amsterdam, where everybody has always done so, obviously does not generate a discontinuity. Cycling in another city where bikes have been long abandoned is quite a different story. The obvious consequence is that a systemic discontinuity must always be evaluated case by case, according to the specificities of the system context.

In the sense we are using it here, social innovation may appear in different ways and places from those we usually consider: on the fringes, more than in the center (meaning in situations considered peripheral, rather than in those that have till now been considered central), bottom-up, more than top-down (meaning in wider society and its networks, rather than in laboratories and the great decision-making centers). For this reason, promising cases of social innovation such as those indicated, though numerous and widespread throughout the world, are often not easily recognizable. What's more, when they are acknowledged they are sometimes actively opposed (because by making a systemic change they modify the economic setup and power balance). On other occasions, when an idea shows great diffusion potential, they become caged in dominant economic models (with the consequent loss of their original social value, as has happened for many proposals in the so-called sharing economy). We shall return to this further in Chapter 4.

Social commons and their regeneration. Various times in the previous paragraphs I have referred to the commons without going into how the term should be understood in this context, but since they are a central part of our discussion, we need to pause briefly and give them a working definition.

The term "commons" refers to a variety of goods fundamental to our existence: some are material and natural, such as water, air, and the environment in general; others are social, such as roads, town squares, public parks, and gardens, but also mutual trust, collaborative capacity, diffuse skills and abilities, perceived security, and others that we shall see later. Traditionally, their existence was never questioned because although they are indispensable, we realize their importance only when they start to disappear. This is what is happening today due to the combined effect of our thoughtless production and consumption and, more recently, the pressure of the neoliberal economy and ideas. Thus it happens that in a world dominated by this economy, by these ideas, and by their pretension to commodify every material and immaterial aspect of our existence, the question of the commons follows a double trajectory. On the one hand, these commons are being eroded and/or commodified to the point where they are being totally consumed, and this unfortunately is still the dominant trend; on the other hand, however, social innovation is creating a countertrend particularly in this field. In the complexity and contradictoriness of contemporary society, strategies are emerging for their regeneration. In other words, a cultural and political movement is growing that recognizes their importance, sees the risk they are running, and is therefore proposing anti-neoliberal policies for their regeneration, and is putting them into practice. I will talk about this policy aspect—policies for everyday life—later on.[9] Here, I would just like to propose a useful definition that helps us understand its nature. In this perspective, I think Carlo Donolo's definition is effective. For this author, the commons are "un insieme di beni necessariamente condivisi. Sono beni in quanto permettono il dispiegarsi della vita sociale, la soluzione di problemi collettivi,

---

[9] The concept of common good has a long story. For years, it has often been used by many authors, including myself, when talking about sustainability. However, it is only recently that it has become for many an all-embracing theme, including every possible strategy for the future. First came Elinor Ostrom, with her studies and her Nobel Prize for economy in 2009. Later came other writers, like Stefano Rodotà, Silke Helfrich, Michel Bauwens, David Bollier, Gregorio Arena, Christian Iaione, and Sheila Foster, who introduced it to the public debate and to that on social innovation. As far as I am concerned, the decisive meeting on these themes was in Bologna, in 2015, in the ambits of a conference, *The City as a Commons*, which was the first theme conference on urban commons held by the International Association for the Study of the Commons (IASC). Elinor Ostrom, *Governing the Commons. The Evolution of Institutions for Collective Action* (Cambridge: Cambridge University Press, 1990); Michel Bauwens, "Towards the Partner State Model of Commons Governance"; Gregorio Arena and Christian Iaione, *L'età della condivisione. La collaborazione tra cittadini e amministrazione per i beni comuni* (Carrocci Editore: Roma, 2015).

la sussistenza dell'uomo nei suoi rapporti con gli ecosistemi di cui è parte. Sono condivisi in quanto … essi stanno meglio e forniscono le loro migliori qualità quando siano trattati e governati come beni 'in comune', a tutti accessibili, almeno in via di principio."[10]

(This roughly translates as: an array of necessarily shared goods. They are goods in as much as they enable social life and solutions to collective problems to function, and foster the subsistence of humankind in relation to the ecosystems of which it is part. They are shared in as much as … they are at their best and provide their best qualities when they are treated and governed as goods "in common," accessible to all, at least in principle).

This definition shows that to have commons there must be a community. Between the two there is a two-way relation: the commons help "social life to develop," meaning that they feed and regenerate the community. But at the same time, the community governs the commons together and thus, implicitly or explicitly, defines the rules by which to do so. Another important question derives from here: not all public assets are commons, and not all commons are public. A neglected and abandoned piazza is a public asset but is not part of the commons because there is no community to look after it. On the other hand, a neighborhood garden, cared for by the neighborhood itself, is part of the commons even when the land it occupies is private. For instance, the clearing with the great holm oak tree, at the start of this chapter, is not a public asset, but when it becomes the center of a community it becomes part of the commons.

The same two-way relation also occurs for social commons: mutual trust, the ability to collaborate, diffuse skills, perception of security, and others that we will find in the following chapters exist—as all commons do—thanks to a

---

[10] Carlo Donolo, *I beni comuni presi sul serio*, in http://www.labsus.org/2010/05/i-beni-comuni-presi-sul-serio/ accessed on September 30, 2017.

community that creates and regenerates them. At the same time they constitute the warp and weave of every possible social fabric and thus of every community: without them society would literally fall apart. On the other hand, since they too, like all commons, cannot be decreed by law, their existence and quality grow out of a complex assortment of activities, conversations, and projects endowed with regenerative capability.

In the past, in the solid world, when social transformations were slow, social commons emerged "almost naturally" out of the long-term workings of communities. Today, in a fluid world in rapid transformation, traditional communities are dissolving and the new ones emerging are unable to recreate them in the quasi-natural ways of the past. Having understood this, we must now understand whether and how this can happen in other ways, considering the unprecedented nature of these new communities and the ways in which they themselves form and evolve over time.

Openness

People, encounters, and conversations. To continue my reflections and reach the point where I can discuss new communities, I shall start from the participant viewpoint, meaning that of a person who I will refer to from now on as the protagonist of our story.

So, our protagonist is a human being living a fluid everyday life alongside other living beings, whether human or otherwise. I am not taking an anthropocentric approach here. The person I am asking you to imagine is not an abstract, powerful, and rational human being placed at the center of the universe. I am thinking of a real person, situated in a well-defined point of time or space with such visibility of things as is available to him—his emotions, his memories, his generosity, and his egoism—with all the contradictions he carries and generates.

Yet this person is interesting for us because, for all his limits, the world will also be what he and people like him, living together in the same world, will have been able to do—for better or for worse.

Since major economic forces (the market and international finance) and ideological pressure (integralism and racism) seem to dominate over any common sense, it becomes an ethical and political choice to start with the people who live in a place together, in the course of their everyday lives, with their problems and their life projects. Such a choice expresses the conviction that, in any case, the world is not a huge machine responding to a unitary logic; it is always the result of different desires and interests and of unpredictable circumstances. Therefore, there is always the possibility of finding spaces where people may think differently. In addition, I believe that it is precisely from the material, everyday dimension of our existence that the possibility of changing things emerges. In a world shaken by the cruel laws of market and finance, and smitten by absurd cries from devotees of racial and religious purity, I believe that the choices each of us makes in everyday life constitute the starting point on which to build a fairer society, one whose existence will not jeopardize the planetary ecosystem and indeed our very humanity.

Of course, we know only too well that human beings can be intolerant, selfish, lazy, and incapable of going beyond their own immediate interests; or they are capable of killing each other for insane reasons. However, we also know that they can be tolerant, active, capable of socializing, of investing their own resources, and even sacrificing themselves for the common good. As I said before, it is an ethical and political choice to call on these positive components of human nature. It is also a forward-looking, proactive choice: each of us may be more or less optimistic about which aspect of human nature may prevail, but if our aim is to collaborate to change the world there is no alternative. It seems to me that this is the only prospect on offer today.

So let's go back to our protagonist. Like all of us he can be described as a living being and also as a social being.[11] This means that while he breathes, he eats and reproduces, or as he thinks, he talks and carries on relationships. Obviously the two descriptions refer to the same entity, but they are also autonomous descriptions (i.e., they are not different ways of saying the same thing): the living being collocates in the space-time of biology and lives in a physical environment (and produces physical environment). The social being collocates in the symbolic-linguistic domain of sociology and lives in language (and generates new language).

Whereas the first dimension constitutes the necessary condition for the second (because to think and talk, there must be a biological organism in a physical environment), it is the second condition that enables the first to exist for human beings. What we call reality is actually something that, for us, exists only to the extent that there is an observer who describes it. Thus, it cannot be separated from the language the observer uses, from the conversations he takes part in, and, ultimately, from the social forms he creates.

Let's pause then on this concept, which I have already used but without giving it a definition. By social forms, we mean meshes of interweaving relationships between people, which acquire recognizable characteristics[12] when they last

---

[11] This way of seeing things owes much to Humbert R. Maturana and Francesco J. Varela. Humbert R. Maturana and Francisco J. Varela, *Autopoiesis and Cognition: The Realization of the Living* (Dordrecht, NDL: Reidel Publishing Company, 1980); H. R. Maturana, "Ontology of Observing: The Biological Foundations of Self-Consciousness and the Physical Domain of Existence," in R. E. Donaldson (ed.), *Texts in Cybernetic Theory: An In-Depth Exploration of the Thought of Humberto Maturana, William T. Powers, and Ernst von Glasersfeld. American Society for Cybernetics (ASC)*. Available at http://cepa. info/597.

[12] Georg Simmel (1858–1918) was a German sociologist whose studies pioneered the concept of social structure. He was a key precursor of social network analysis.

long enough. Thus the term "social form" has a very wide meaning. It includes institutionalized social forms, such as families, business companies, and state apparatuses, and also various kinds of informal communities: those non-institutionalized social forms that form the connective fabric of every society. So, a community too may be described as a mesh of interweaving conversations, and its nature will depend on the types of conversation taking place within it and what sparks them. On the other hand, since we converse about the world (about the state of things) and about how to change the world (about how the state of things could change), communities are also connected in various ways to issues (communities of interest) or to actions (communities of purpose). In addition, there are communities that exist within the ambit of consolidated traditions and those that exist by choice: intentional communities, which one is free to enter and equally free to leave.

If we consider the life of our protagonist, he cannot be described without reference to the encounters he has and the conversations he engages in, which constitute his social environment.

A word of caution is needed, however, before I go on: I cannot continue my reflections referring to every possible social form to be found in the world. So, I will limit the field to those that exist in the fluid, connected world I started with. I know very well that this condition is not valid for everybody and certainly not for everybody in the same way, but it is the only choice I can make: like the protagonist, I cannot move outside the point of view and action in which I find myself living. However, I hope that these reflections from my point of observation may shed light on the differences and stimulate autonomous reflection in those who find themselves adopting other points of view and action on the world.

Thus the protagonist of our story is a person who is part of a fluid, connected society, living the crises and transformations it is undergoing. This is a condition that is no longer confined to certain geographical areas but extends to all sectors of society that have adopted it, adapting certain aspects to fit the specifics of the local situation.

Community as a space of opportunity. The term "community" still generally evokes images of a closed social form, connected to a place and characterized by a dense, stable, and long-lasting network of ties, toward which we may all nurture different sentiments that oscillate between nostalgia and a sense of claustrophobia. We can talk about it, but the fact is that this type of closed community, rooted in a place and stable in time, barely exists now. Where they still remain, they are in crisis and/or changing into something else. Of course, this does not mean that there are not, or will not be, other forms of community. Quite the opposite, in recent years the number of social forms that we call communities, rightly or wrongly, has been growing, but that particular form of traditional community cannot return. What has happened? How did it happen?

The immediate answer is familiar: breaking the constraints of spatial proximity (firstly with developments in transport and then in telecommunications) has changed the way communities exist and with it the relationship between people and places. The result is that actors in modernized societies find themselves living in a context where the possibility for interaction between subjects (and thus the possibility for a community to exist) is no longer limited by the need for spatial proximity between interlocutors. Since it is possible to communicate irrespective of distance, communities refer to places that are not necessarily physical, circumscribed, and contiguous; each of us may be part of a multiplicity of social forms, engaging in conversations with various widely scattered interlocutors.

Thus, everyday life has become very different from the premodern past: we work in faraway places with different time schedules; our children do not go to the same schools; we marry people whose families do not know each other and when we die, no longer do we all go to the same cemeteries. The result is that communities, as they were traditionally understood, have fallen apart. The closed groups open up and society seems to consist of individuals who, living in the current technological environment as they are, have become connected individuals,[13] free of the previous social ties but connected by social media and the internet. They are individuals who engage in a variety of conversations of different kinds, and in so doing they dissolve the previous communities (premodern communities and those that were formed in the last century) and produce unprecedented social forms: there are individuals who are connected but solitary, with a tendency to remain closed in their information bubbles; by reaction, there are nostalgic communities, harking back to an imaginary past and confined within their asphyxiating localism; and there are various combinations of the two. Hence there are new pseudo-communities through which people attempt, though rarely with success, to escape their solitude, fear, and crisis of identity. Fortunately, as I have already stated, there are also the new communities produced by social innovation and which in themselves produce innovation. They are a concrete indication that there can be a new idea of community befitting a fluid, connected environment, and despite their diversity, communities produced by innovation do have characterizing traits that distinguish them from other social forms.

The possibility of choosing. These new communities should be seen as a mesh of interweaving conversations in which people take part in different ways, choosing where, how, and for how long to allocate their resources (attention, skills, and relational availability). The first characteristic that distinguishes them from premodern communities is that the ties created within them are the result of a choice, so we are talking about intentional communities. One aspect, however, also distinguishes them

---

[13] Barry Wellman, "Little Boxes, Glocalization, and Networked Individualism," pp. 11–25, in Makoto Tanabe, Peter van Den Besselaar, and Toru Ishida (eds.), *Digital Cities II: Computational and Sociological Approaches* (Berlin: Springer-Verlag, 2002).

from the intentional communities of the twentieth century (from political parties, trade unions, and also from the various forms of alternative community that emerged in the last century): their multiple, nonexclusive, reversible character, practicable with various levels of commitment. As a result, those who take part in these communities do not do so to find themselves a ready-made solution and/or identity, but rather to build their own solutions and identity through the choices and negotiations it puts into effect. It follows, then, that the larger the number and the wider the diversity of opportunities for encounters and action they offer, the more important they will be for their members.

A space of opportunity. These new communities can be described as spaces of opportunity that offer possibilities for expression and comparison, where solutions are looked for to problems, and that are open toward new prospects. They are therefore defined by the quantity and quality of the conversations active within them. These can be conversations with no practical aim, or they may be geared to action. In the latter case, they may be actions in which someone does something for someone else or in which everybody participates on the same level, focusing on a result and collaborating to achieve it. Ultimately, on a molecular level, contemporary communities are characterized by the quality and density of the conversations, and thus of the encounters, that occur in them and the capacity of their members to transform these into actions capable of achieving shared results.

Piece-by-piece community building. Because they consist of interweaving conversations, and thus of encounters between people, the new communities cannot be designed as if they were organic entities. Instead, what needs creating is the space of opportunity, mentioned previously, in which not only can a variety of encounters and conversations occur, but they can also be encouraged to evolve in the best possible way. For contemporary communities, it would seem that the expression *community building* should be taken literally: communities are built from their molecular elements, meaning from the various types of encounter between people, and between people and places, that constitute the relational material they are made of. Thus, community building corresponds to creating opportunities for people to meet and enhancing the quality of these encounters.

Continual regeneration. Community building never finishes. As discussed earlier, in a fluid world the stability of the forms is always associated with the continuity of the surrounding conditions that generated them. Thus, on conclusion of the initial stage of community building in the strict sense, it moves on to the management stage. However, this requires not only the minor interventions to ensure continuity of functioning that are normally implied by the term but also ongoing activities geared to maintaining the conditions required for the community's long-term existence. This calls for periodic initiatives that revitalize the community, bringing new life and ensuring continuity of commitment and generational turnover.

The existence of designing coalitions. The new communities emerge and live, thanks to the existence of particularly proactive, motivated people within them with a considerable degree of mutual understanding. Together, they form designing coalitions that, whether formally or de facto, try to put their collaboratively produced ideas into practice and keep them going. Such coalitions may be horizontal peer groups (when the skills and powers necessary to put what they are trying to achieve into practice lie within the group) or mixed (when they need to call on skills and powers that are not available within the group of people directly involved in order to achieve their aims). The relationship between this more active group and the other members of the community is obviously a delicate question—one that is very important for defining the character of the community itself and its long-term evolution.

A hybrid environment. All these new communities live in hybrid, online–offline environments. Nevertheless, the way they do so enables us to distinguish two large families: communities of purpose supported by a digital platform that facilitates the various activities (scheduling meetings, circulating information, and coordinating activities) and communities of interest based on a digital platform that enables a large number of individuals to get in contact and which can activate them around a particular theme (activity proposals, an event, a project). Without the platform they would have had no way of meeting, comparing experiences, and producing shared knowledge and visions. Experience also tells us that both communities of purpose and communities of interest are important: the former without the latter would risk remaining a place of discussion about theories and principles without the possibility of impacting on practice. Vice versa, a community of purpose without a community of interest to refer to would risk not having an adequate background of ideas and experiences to prevent them making mistakes that a wider knowledge of the issue could help them avoid. Similarly, it could help prevent them setting off along trajectories that might lead to them losing the social and cultural values from which the idea emerged.

Continuity of place. What has been said so far about the new communities also has considerable implications as far as the evolution of the idea of place is concerned. A place is a space endowed with meaning. On the other hand, since the meaning is a result of human conversations, we can also say that a place is a space where there are people who have reasons for talking about it. So, in practice, it is a space inhabited by a community interested in the place where they live. As anticipated, the discussion about places is linked to that about communities.

For premodern communities this interaction was simple and immediately recognizable: communities were stable and based on a dense mesh of strong ties associated with activities that took place in the same physical space. Thus, they produced equally stable places, dense with meaning. In the fluid world, things are no longer like that. The new communities also collocate in space and produce a place but because their space is hybrid, physical-virtual space, the places they produce are also hybrid and endowed with meanings that are as light and variable as the ties of the conversations that generated them.

The crisis in communities and places that we perceive today is therefore not linked to their disappearance, but rather to the transformation they have undergone and particularly to the implications of their hybrid, physical-virtual character. We could ask whether and to what extent this hybrid nature of the new communities, and the places they create, really constitutes a problem, or whether what many people see as a crisis is not just the difficulty of adapting to something new and nostalgia for the places and communities of a (more or less imaginary) past. My opinion is that it is not only a question of nostalgia and lack of adaptation. I believe that we are faced with a real difficulty and that the more the virtual components in communities and places prevail, the greater the difficulty will be. I believe this for various reasons, some of which are very practical (and are therefore quite separate from our cultural resistance to what is new).

While it is true that there are activities that can be carried out at a distance and online, there are many others that cannot be. For example, let's consider care activities in the widest sense of the term: care for the sick, for children, and for the elderly, and also care in the sense of mutual support in moments of difficulty. It is evident that at least a part of the relationships that occur in this context must have a physical dimension and one of proximity: we may be part of numerous social networks, that is, online communities, but when we need somebody for something concrete, that person is not there. We find ourselves completely alone. Not recognizing that, in their everyday lives, people also live in their physical dimension and that for a number of reasons physical proximity is crucial, leads to dehumanizing visions and proposals. One of the most emblematic is that of an elderly person alone in an intelligent house in the company of a robot.

Similar considerations can be made for the environment and its problems: the health of a territory, its resilience to catastrophic events, its maintenance, and even its aesthetic quality require a community that takes care of it.[14] If the people who live there are part of the prevalent virtual communities, referring to virtual environments, they tend to reduce their ties with the place where they live to a minimum. In the end, they fail to take care of it. Of course, the interruption in care for the environment does not depend only on the diffusion of networks and communities online: neglected peripheral areas of cities, hydro-geological disasters in abandoned hillside areas, and social fragility in the face of catastrophic events also depend on other sociocultural dynamics. However, it is certain that the evolution of social networks toward virtual forms collaborates in this process of territorial abandonment. It should be said, though, that this highly negative result of the diffusion of the internet and digital technology is not inevitable. On the contrary, as we shall see, they can also contribute to the regeneration of communities and care for local areas.

To move in this direction, it is therefore necessary to update not only the concept of community but also that of interaction between communities and places. We must shift from one mental image to another: from that of an inward-looking community and place to that of a variety of communities living different types of space and thus producing different types of places. So, if we also want to have communities linked to places, we need

---

[14] The concept of resilience comes up several times in this book, so it needs to be defined more carefully. Resilience is the capability of a system to cope with stress and failure without breaking down and, more importantly in relation to socio-technical systems, to learn from experience. For this reason, it should be considered a fundamental characteristic of any future society. Recently, we have been hearing resilience talked about with increasing frequency when confronted with various crises and catastrophic events that have made the vulnerability of our contemporary society more and more apparent. Therefore, precisely because the use of the term has become so widespread, its meaning must be carefully discussed and understood (see also E. Manzini, "Error-Friendliness: How to Design Resilient Socio-technical Systems," in Jon Goofbun (ed.), *Scarcity: Architecture in an Age of Depleting Resources* (Hoboken: Wiley, 2012).

to create the conditions for this to happen: in other words, we need communities in which conversations are face to face and that also have reasons for looking after the environment they live in. It is not so difficult: any purpose community whose aim involves people doing something together in the physical world (sharing spaces, cultivating the same garden, collaborating in the care of children and the elderly) will necessarily talk about the environment in which it is happening, thus contributing to transforming it into a place.

When a community operates in this way, in order to stress its place-producing role, we could call it a *community of place:* a community of purpose whose raison d'être includes looking after the place it finds itself in. Like all contemporary communities, it is an open, light, intentional community. The same is true for the place it produces, which does not exist simply because "it has always existed" but because someone has intentionally done something to make it exist. In other words, intentional communities produce intentional places.

Lightness

Meaningful encounters and their enabling ecosystems. How are communities of place built? How are occasions created for face-to-face encounters where people weave relationships among themselves and with the place where they live? How can this happen in a society where people are always involved at a distance in delocalized, virtual social networks, and even those living nearby have little possibility to meet up (because their schedules and lifestyles are different)? This kind of question motivated a design-research program called Cultures of Resilience (CoR),[15] run by the University of the Arts London

---

[15] Cultures of Resilience (CoR) has been a research project developed by the University of the Arts London between 2014 and 2016. Its aim was to build a multiple vision of the role of culture in the creation of resilient systems.

from 2014 to 2016. The program included projects carried out in London by various teams of university teachers and students who focused on and discussed the way in which complete strangers had met and shared an activity. Coherently with the idea of community expounded in the previous paragraphs, it was agreed that these encounters, which were called *meaningful encounters*, were the molecular elements from which to start building new communities. The thirteen projects that became the focus of attention had different themes derived from different approaches, including a neighborhood library, a support service for young people with mental problems, activities in prisons, and artistic performances with elderly people. However, some common traits emerged from these very different initiatives.

The first group of observations confirmed what all the experiences of social innovation design have shown: it is not possible to design interactions between people directly and bring them into being. Instead, conditions can be made more favorable for them to emerge by creating artifacts dedicated to making them possible and probable. This can be done in two ways: by creating support systems for well-defined activities (in technical terms, by creating enabling systems)[16] or by making the whole environment more favorable to an unspecified

---

Coordinated by Ezio Manzini and Jeremy Till, the project involved a team of over twenty teachers and researchers. In its second stage, it examined thirteen projects carried out by as many research teams in collaboration with various social actors in different zones of London. One of the outcomes of the research path was the discussion about the way these projects had helped to connect people and people with the places. Some of the results of these activities can be found in Ezio Manzini and Jeremy Till, *Cultures of Resilience* (London: Hato Press, 2015) (http://culturesofresilience.org/wp-content/uploads/resources/CoR-Booklet-forHomePrinting.pdf) and on the website http://culturesofresilience.org. and in: Manzini Ezio, and Adam Thorp. "Weaving People and Places: Art and Design for Resilient Communities." *She Ji: The Journal of Design, Economies, and Innovation* 4, no. 1 (2018): 1–9. DOI: https://doi.org/10.1016/j.sheji.2018.03.003.

[16] Ezio Manzini, *Design, When Everybody Designs* (Cambridge, MA: MIT Press, 2015), p. 167.

variety of encounters, conversations, and actions (technically, by creating infrastructure, i.e., by infrastructuring[17]).

At first glance, most of the CoR projects seemed to have adopted the first approach. However, on a closer look, the situation appears more complex: what has been achieved for a specific project (products, services, dedicated places) can later be used in other projects, thus becoming part of the material infrastructure of a space. Likewise, the relational values produced by specific actions tend to remain in the community where they were produced, becoming social commons, so they form the relational component of the infrastructure available to a community to regenerate itself. It follows that a virtuous circle may develop between the two approaches: development of the infrastructure makes the birth and diffusion of new collaborative projects more probable. Vice versa, the birth and diffusion of new projects, with the relational value they produce, create commons that become part of a better relational infrastructure (obviously the reverse is also true: failure to create relational value in certain encounters may induce skepticism that may spread and accumulate in the environment, making it less favorable for future initiatives). Generalizing on these observations, we can say that encounters, conversations, and actions happen in a socio-technical ecosystem in which two-way ties are created (virtuous or vicious circles) between the quality of the single encounters and the quality of the environment they are in.

In the second group of observations, a closer look was taken at the quality of the encounters the projects made possible. This particularly concerned the way in which encounters came about between different interlocutors who, at least initially, did not know each other. Many members of the project

---

[17] Pelle Ehn, "Participation in Design Things," in *Proceedings of Participatory Design Conference* (Bloomington, Indiana: Indiana University Press, 2008), p. 4.

team observed that these encounters took place outside the participants' normal comfort zone. It was as if it was necessary for everybody in the same way to be in an unfamiliar situation. The lesson we can draw from this is that for strangers to meet and establish a real relationship, everyone must be in the same boat—all feeling the same conditions of vulnerability (there must not be some who feel at home, while others do not). Besides, it is precisely that acceptance of risk when opening up to a stranger, and thus becoming in some way vulnerable, that gives the encounter a relational value. Indeed, establishing a relationship means opening up and therefore becoming vulnerable.[18]

It generates a tension between two opposing inclinations: on the one hand, we would like encounters with relational qualities; and on the other, we are worried about the commitment they call for and the vulnerability they produce.

The projects in question developed different strategies for dealing with these contradictions but with one common trait: they all tried to combine the condition of vulnerability with the offer of some kind of protection. So, they activated the encounters by creating conditions of mutual vulnerability, but they made them happen in safe places (de-risked places, as the project teams called them): protected environments, where "risk taking" could become acceptable for the actors involved.

This observation tells us something new about the characteristics of enabling systems: if we are looking to make encounters possible and probable that are also meaningful (in the sense that they may lead to collaborative actions) and of high quality (in the sense that they produce relational values), we must have the sensitivity to balance a sense of openness

---

[18] Carla M. Cipolla, "Tourist or Guest—Designing Tourism Experiences or Hospitality Relations?," in Anne-Marie Willis (ed.), *Design Philosophy Papers: Collection Two* (Ravensbourne, Australia: Team D/E/S Publications, 2004) (https://doi.org/10.2752/144871304X13966215067912).

toward the other person (and the ensuing vulnerability) with a sense of protection. There is no fixed rule as to how to do this. We *simply* have to bring into play an appropriate sensitivity and design culture.

Encounters with strangers. To conclude, we can highlight another lesson that we can draw from the CoR program and that we can sum up in the expression: *give value to lightness*. The projects discussed were all copromoted by a school. Therefore, the workgroups always included students: community members whose role meant that their membership was inevitably temporary. In the first place, this was seen as a limit to the project and its potential results. However, once the issue was clearly in focus, it became apparent that communities that included transitory citizens—in our case they were students, but they could equally well have been temporary project-workers, tourists, or migrants—were far from being an exception. Thus, the cases in question and the encounters they generated could be seen as emblematic of a society, in which an increasing number of people are on the move for various reasons, and, consequently, in which encounters between strangers and encounters that we know will be short-lived should be considered the new norm.

The question we then asked ourselves and which I am asking again now is the following: Can these brief encounters between strangers contribute to the building of a community of place? If so, what is their quality? The CoR research team gave a positive answer: brief encounters too can have relational qualities and can be connected to a place. In addition, they can help more stable residents to understand how to include people on the move—meaning new or transitory residents—in the existent local community, thus making it more dynamic and open. This observation, which in our case emerged out of practical experience, can be generalized. With reference to Mark Granovetter's conceptualization, we know that in a complex society, weak ties play a fundamental role: they make the entire system more open and able to communicate. When there are too few weak ties, writes Granovetter, "information is self-contained and experiences are not exchanged."[19] This is why I think my summary of the CoR project in the expression "give value to lightness" is appropriate. I believe that the value of lightness is the key to understanding (and contributing to producing) community in a fluid world: new communities, based on interactions that are open to the new and the unknown, that are light and flexible produce relational value.

The value of lightness. I believe that the idea of lightness proposed here may be a useful stimulus in the discussion on new communities. However, to make it so, we must give the term "lightness" a deeper connotation than that often attributed to it. To clarify what I mean, we can look at the meaning given to it by Italo Calvino in his *Six Memos for the Next Millennium*. In this book, published in 1988, Calvino proposed five words that expressed the qualities he would have liked for the twenty-first century. The first is lightness. Calvino wrote twenty-five pages to say what this meant for him and with reference to literature. As many and maybe more would be necessary to say what this term might mean for the encounters, conversations, and communities that we would like to see emerge in a fluid world. But one sentence from Calvino can help us to say it more concisely here. To introduce his point of view on lightness, Calvino made reference to *De rerum natura* by the Roman philosopher Lucretius and wrote "it is the first great work of poetry in which knowledge of the world tends to dissolve the solidity of the world, leading to a perception of all that is infinitely minute, light and mobile ... the poetry of the invisible, of infinite unexpected possibilities."[20] The encounters

---

[19] Mark Granovetter, "The Strength of Weak Ties," *American Journal of Sociology* 78, no. 6 (1973), 1360–1380.

Joon Baeck, "A Socio-Technical Framework for Collaborative Services: Designing a Digital Platform for Collaborative Communities," doctoral thesis, Politecnico di Milano, February 2011.

[20] Italo Calvino, *Six Memos for the Next Millennium* (Cambridge: Harvard University Press, 1988), pp. 8 and 9 (English version).

and conversations that give rise to light communities, in the sense that Calvino uses the term, are therefore those that give a deep perception of what is minute, light, and mobile: of what makes visible that which is not so and of that which opens up new possibilities.

Calvino rightly says that the fact that he has discussed the quality of lightness does not mean that weight does not have value and quality. It only means that he has more to say about lightness. The same is true for the encounters we are talking about. Light encounters are not the only ones that may enrich a space of opportunities. However, they are the ones that are newer and more probable today and whose unprecedented nature needs to be understood better.

2

Life Projects: Autonomy and Collaboration

It's evening and I am at home. On the television news, I am watching people arriving from the sea with a light of hope in their eyes—hope for a new life. A story comes to mind that I know well, and I have been told about it many times at home. Mine is a family of refugees from Istria. In 1945, my parents had to leave their home in Pola and take a boat across the sea to somewhere else, where they hoped life would be better. They were forced to go, but to do so they had to come up with an idea and find the means to make it come true. In short, they had to decide on a project: a great life project that set all that came after on a different course. For this, when I watch those people coming off the ships that picked them up, I cannot but think that each of them is there because, driven by necessity like my parents, they have imagined a project and set it in motion: their life project.

Of course, not everyone driven to move by the unliveable situation in their place of origin does so with a project. People fleeing from war and hunger who follow a flow and end up in a refugee camp have had no choice. Other people and events have decided for them. Theirs is effectively a deportation: a change of life context entirely directed by others. However, it is not the same for people who themselves organize their journey across Africa and the sea to reach Europe. Just as it was for my parents, they have a vision and have put together the means to achieve it or at least to try to do so.

There are various reasons for starting with this empathetic glance at migrants to frame a discussion on life projects. The first is that I am unable to say or write anything these days without reference to the issue that, for me, is a clear indicator of the catastrophes underway and our present inability to deal with them. The second pertains entirely to the contents of this book. For me, these two contrasting images of uprootedness—migrants who design, or try to design, their new living conditions and deported people who endure what is imposed on them—seem emblematic of a more general existential state: a general uprootedness, produced not only by people on the move but also by the crises of places, communities and former ways of being and thinking. From here stems the need to design one's own life autonomously in order to avoid deportation to the concentration and control camps of the twenty-first century, which range from refugee camps (with which the world is tragically filling itself) to the run-down urban fringes, protected residences, and information bubbles we are driven into.[1]

Project-making

Projects, designers, and design capability. In the 1980s and 1990s, sociologists like Ulrich Beck, Anthony Giddens,

---

[1] In my experience, the need to rethink the migrant issue—not only to deal with the urgent problems that are arising but also to trigger wider rethinking about the conditions of all the inhabitants of contemporary metropolises—emerged in the ambits of *Reframing Migration*, a program of activities that took place in London in 2015–2016, promoted by DESIS UAL Lab and SILK-Social Innovation Lab Kent. Some of the results can be found in Emma Barrett and Carla Cipolla, Reframing Migration, DESIS Network, 2016 (http://www.desisnetwork.org/wp-content/uploads/2016/10/Reframing-Migration-REPORT_2016.pdf).

and Scott Lash[2] argued that in modernity, traditions were evaporating and with them were disappearing the conventions that until then had guided peoples' lives. Consequently, everyone had to make their own life choices, meaning that they had to design their own everyday lives and indeed their entire life stories. More than twenty years later, this existential condition and its effects have become even more visible than they were then. In particular, the effort that it involves has emerged all too clearly, with the frustrations it so often generates and the resulting drive not to choose autonomously, but rather to adopt one of the prepackaged life stories that are imposed on us today.

In order to discuss these issues further, it is useful to introduce some of the concepts in common use but which lend themselves to various interpretations. I'm referring in particular to the very ideas of "project" and "design" and their associated terms "designer" and "design capability." I have already dealt with these elsewhere, but I believe it is useful to look again at some of the main points.[3] The concept of "project" is a fertile one, and over time, it has lent itself to many definitions in different cultural ambits. For me, in this context, a project is a sequence of conversations and actions on the world, the aim of which is to bring it closer to the way we would like it to be. Doing this entails designing: making a critical evaluation of the state of

---

[2] In the 1990s, these three authors introduced the concept of "reflexive modernity," which contains many of the issues I refer to in this book, and discussed how they have evolved. Some of their works referred to are Ulrich Beck, *What Is Globalization?* (Cambridge: Polity Press, 1999); Ulrich Beck, *Risk Society: Towards a New Modernity* (New Delhi: Sage, 1992) (Translated from the German *Risikogesellschaft* 1986); Anthony Giddens, *Consequences of Modernity* (Cambridge: Polity Press, 1990); Anthony Giddens, *The Third Way: The Renewal of Social Democracy* (Cambridge: Polity, 1998); Scott Lash, *Global Modernities* (Thousand Oaks, CA: Sage, 1995).

[3] The issues dealt with in these paragraphs were examined in depth in my book *Design, When Everybody Designs. An Introduction to Design for Social Innovation* (MIT Press, 2015). That book discussed these issues from the point of view of design experts. Here, the point of view is that of nonexperts who are nevertheless involved in the need to confront life with a design attitude.

things, imagining how we would like them to be, and having the necessary relational system and tools at hand to transform them—and all this in terms of both their practical functioning (problem-solving) and their meaning (sense-making).

From these definitions of project and designing derives a definition of "designer" as "project maker" in the sense that anyone doing what I have just said can be seen as a project maker. In this connotation, a designer is any subject, whether individual or collective, at the moment in which they consciously intervene on the world, meaning they are aware of their own intentions and the field of possibility available to them (in reality, neither the intentions nor the fields of possibility are ever totally clear. However, we shall come back to this later). This definition of designer is very wide and includes not only those who operate institutionally as such (I will refer to them as design experts) but also those who are not experts but who nevertheless act in the way described. Using the conceptualization introduced in the previous chapter, it follows that a person who designs is a person who takes part in a variety of conversations (and thus of social forms) and operates on the physical and biological environment of his living context adopting strategies that, as we shall see, are his life projects.

If each of us can do this, it is because, as human beings, we are endowed with *design capability:* a complex capability that in turn results from the combination of various capabilities proper to humans. These are *critical sense* (which enables us to see what is unacceptable in the situation we are in), *creativity* (by which we imagine how things could be), the *ability to analyze* (to recognize and assess the limits of the system and the resources available), and *practical sense* (by which we put action strategies into effect that, within the limits of the system and making best use of the resources available, enable us to approach what we had imagined). Obviously, like all the others, the resulting design capability is not the same for everybody and, above all, to be usable when we really need it, it has to be exercised. In other words, design capability is like singing: all of us can do it, not everyone has the same gift, but if we practice we can all sing in a choir.

Having said this, we must stress that wide as the range of activities may be that come under this definition of design, it cannot cover the whole universe of human actions on the world. Many of them we carry out unconsciously, routinely, within tried and tested conventions, or with reference to such a limited field of possibility that there is no freedom of choice. All these activities are not design and the person doing them, in that moment at least, is not a designer. The difference between actions on the world that are design and those that are not is of great importance in relation to the questions I intend to discuss here and thus requires further elaboration.

The crisis of the conventional mode. The world we live in has, to a large extent, been constructed by us and endowed with the meanings we give it. This has always happened in two main ways: one conventional, the other by design.

In the *conventional mode*, things are done and interpreted following rules, with reference to meaning systems that have evolved and are handed down through the workings of generation after generation of human beings. These conventions constitute an implicit expertise, acquired by initiation (emulating a master). They allow results to be achieved by doing "as it has always been done" (with no need for explanation) and are acquired by the entire community. This means that within the community everyone involved in the action will almost naturally agree on what to do, without the need for rules and meanings to be clearly explained, and without anybody in the conversation and the action thinking that there might be alternative ways of doing what they are doing.[4]

---

[4] Implicit or tacit knowledge is part of the material culture of a society. It is handed down from master to apprentice by emulation, with no formal, explicit learning. Reflection on this term has followed various threads. The one that was fundamental for me was initiated by André Leroi-Gourhan, with his book

Like all human constructs, conventions evolve with time. However, they do so slowly by subsequent adjustment, without the need to call into question the entire sense frame in which they occur. Consequently, although to all intents and purposes on a wider timescale they are cognitive artifacts that depend on human action, on the scale at which we live, they would appear to be indisputable: a set of rules taken as a quasi-natural given. We should add that as long as it works, the conventional mode seems to be very effective: it enables various questions to be dealt with quickly (doing "as has always been done") and efficiently (since it incorporates the experience of many previous generations). However, to function, conventions need a fundamental precondition: the questions and problems to be dealt with must be stable in the long term (or change very slowly) to allow the entire community concerned to accumulate the tacit knowledge required to cope with them. This tacit knowledge may rest on centuries of history (like the ancient skills of craftsmanship from long ago or the rituals of everyday life in premodern culture). Alternatively, the knowledge may be more recently acquired but which has still had the time to become embedded in society, giving rise to the new traditions that emerged in the last century (such as the artisanship based on new materials and technologies that appeared in that period or new rituals and behavior that emerged during those years). Eric Hobsbawm writes: "'Traditions' which appear or claim to be

(or. fr. André Leroi-Gourhan, *Le geste et la parole. Technique et langage* (Paris: Editions Albin Michel, 1964) (Copyright © 1964 Editions Albin Michel).

For Leroi-Gourhan, implicit knowledge is incorporated in the activities of those who have it, becoming a quasi-natural extension of their own ability. Instead, Michael Polanyi and, in a different way, Ikujiro Nonaka and Hirotaka Takeuchi have highlighted the complex relationship between what they call "tacit knowledge" and "explicit knowledge." Michael Polanyi, *The Tacit Dimension* (New York: Anchor Books, 1966); Ikujiro Nonaka and Hirotaka Takeuchi, *The Knowledge Creating Company* (Oxford University Press, 1995).

old are often quite recent in origin and sometimes invented."[5] It is true, and the many examples that Hobsbawm cites prove it very clearly. However, for these new traditions too, the context must be sufficiently stable for them to last. When everything changes rapidly, they too tend to dissolve and lose their capacity to orient people's lives and work. At the end of the day, whenever there is insufficient time to accumulate the tacit knowledge required to deal with the problem and solve it, the conventional mode ceases to function and explicit knowledge has to be called into play in design mode.

The two modes, conventional and design, have always existed, but for a long time the former prevailed over the latter. This is true of all application fields: from personal life choices to the building of cathedrals. Then from the Renaissance onward, things began to change. Issues and problems emerged that had never appeared before, and the explicit knowledge of science gradually replaced the tacit knowledge of conventions, and finally physical and digital connectivity has done the rest, leading us to the fluid, accelerated, and—as Anthony Giddens and Scott Lash called it—post-traditional[6] society. In this society, when confronted with new problems and acting in unexplored circumstances, people themselves have to determine, whether they like it or not, what they wish to be and do, and make the appropriate moves to achieve it or at least approach it.

Difficulties, risks, and opportunities. In a post-traditional society, the fluid environment we find ourselves living in can be seen as a mesh of projects. Some are our own expressions of our autonomy—our freedom of choice. Others are not: they are projects thought up and set in motion by others to which

---

[5] Eric Hobsbawm and Terence Ranger (eds.), *The Invention of Traditions* (Cambridge: Cambridge University Press, 1983), p. 1.

[6] Anthony Giddens, "Living in a Post-Traditional Society," in Beck, Giddens, and Lash, *Reflexive Modernization: Politics, Tradition and Aesthetics in the Modern Social Order* (Cambridge: Polity Press, 1994); Scott Lash, *Detraditionalization: Critical Reflections on Authority and Identity* (Cambridge, MA, 1996).

we consciously or unconsciously adhere or are compelled to adhere.

Here, I would like to explore how and when the former, our autonomous life projects, can prevail over the latter, and how and when their development may help us toward a better society and environment. I should say right from the start that however difficult this may seem, I believe it is not impossible. I think that the end of conventions may offer an unprecedented opportunity to set human capabilities free: for single individuals, in terms of their individual freedom, and for society at large, by releasing resources that could potentially become available in the learning process toward sustainability.

To argue my case, I shall start by considering those who think otherwise and see the spread of the design mode in everyday life as an expression of the colonization of our lives and minds by neoliberalism. The Korean philosopher Byung-Chul Han, living in Germany, writes that in the neoliberalist world "we exploit ourselves voluntarily under the illusion that we are fulfilling ourselves. Not the suppression of liberty, but rather its exploitation maximizes productivity and efficiency."[7] In the world that Han describes, we are driven to use entrepreneurship, creativity, and therefore the design capability available to us, to exploit ourselves, very often inflicting on ourselves impracticable projects and then feeling guilty because of the results we are unable to achieve (results that we had apparently chosen freely, but which had actually been cunningly imposed on us by the dominant culture).

Of course, I can see all this too. I can also see that this performance stress tends to drive many people out of the game and toward self-marginalization—toward giving up project-making altogether. Alternatively, as discussed earlier, it may

---

[7] Byung-Chul Han, *L'espulsione dell'Altro* (Nottetempo: Milano, 2017), p. 25; Vedi anche, *Psychopolitik: Neoliberalismus und die neuen Machttechniken* (Fischer, Frankfurt, 2014)—trad. Federica Buongiorno, *Psicopolitica* (Nottetempo, 2016).

lead them to adopt as their own a life project proposed by others (neoliberalist, as Han describes, or a neo-authoritarian reaction to it, the most dramatic examples of the latter being religious fundamentalism and reactionary populism). So, I am very worried too. However, my interpretation of the overall framework is different: the problem underlying the social disaster outlined above does not lie in the fact that people are driven to make projects, but in how they do so—that is, in the fact that they are not in a condition to do it well (which means to do it well for themselves *and* for society as a whole). The main reason for this is not the lack of personal capabilities, but it is the number of difficulties created by the contexts in which they live. Contexts that, very often, not only do not support them but make their life more difficult and lead them in wrong directions.

To counteract this drift, we need to separate the long-standing process by which people find themselves having to use their design capability more frequently from the way in which this actually occurs in practice. In other words, I believe that neoliberalism has appropriated a process already in progress and shaped it to its own interests, thus proposing and disseminating an idea of life project that is detrimental in its aims and methods. Underlying the sad situation of millions of people who race and compete to achieve results that have never really been called into question is the functionalist, efficiency-based approach to designing that was the norm in the last century. This was adopted by neoliberal thinking, instilling the idea that everybody must design and plan their own lives to achieve an idea of well-being determined by a few, uncontested parameters: money, success, power, and physical prowess. The quality of such a project is judged by the degree of efficiency with which its objectives are achieved. It is an incremental project (one that does not call the existing systems into question), solitary (one that does not oppose the dominant hyper-individualism) and that, because of this, is almost always destined to failure. There is also the even sadder situation of millions of other people who, when confronted with the difficulties, failures, and frustrations it may lead to, decide to opt out and, instead, enlarge the army of the disheartened and of those who decide to adhere to reactionary and authoritarian projects based on a simplification of reality.

However, adopting a design approach to one's own life may lead in directions that are rather different from these. It may start by redefining the sense of things, and it may pose objectives that break with the dominant line of reasoning. It may choose to slow down, to move outside the rules of the game, to collaborate with others instead of competing, and to look at them with empathy rather than seeing them as potential enemies. The projects that emerge may open new prospects and invent futures in contrast with the sterile, caged-in future usually proposed. When looking at the way things are going in the world, this position may seem naive. Maybe it is. Yet I still think that not recognizing that there may also be an opportunity in this spread of designing means losing a historical occasion. Furthermore, the wave of social innovation mentioned in the previous chapter shows us that this is not merely wishful thinking; it tells us that it is possible, and that, indeed, many are actually doing it, by developing projects quite independently of the mind-set and praxis of the great dominant projects.

Projects, autonomy, and new conventions. So, what does "autonomous project" mean in the current context?[8] In practical terms, it means breaking with dominant ideas and behaviors, moving outside the rules of the game, and deciding

---

[8] A discussion is currently underway about the meaning of the term "autonomy" when collocated with that of "project." In the call for papers for a special issue of *SDRJ* (*Strategic Design Research Journal*), Chiara del Gaudio, Andrea Botero, and Alfredo Gutierrez Borrero write: 'Building on the idea of autonomía, we ask ourselves: What is the relation between autonomía, design practices and the political activation of relational and communal logics and ways of being, in current research and design practice?' (Call for papers: Autonomía | Design strategies for enabling design process, Special Issue of *SDRJ*, 2017).

to collaborate with others. In other words, it means adopting ways of thinking and doing things that contrast with prevailing ones in the context we find ourselves in.

Before discussing about how and when this may happen, one point needs clarification. For human beings, autonomy does not, indeed cannot, mean closing in on oneself: the thinking and the actions that determine any project grow out of interweaving conversations—action-oriented conversations in particular. Projects endowed with autonomy grow out of conversations that apply the human capabilities of critical analysis, creativity, and openness toward the world and possible futures. For this reason, designing in autonomy means taking part in conversations that use these capabilities to imagine actions and results that are largely independent of the general context in which we find ourselves living and operating. When this does not occur, it means that the conversations we are taking part in do not express this capacity for critical analysis and, whether intentionally or otherwise, we are adhering to life projects thought up for us by others.

Admittedly, choosing, and therefore imagining and setting in motion life projects, is a hard struggle in terms of the time and attention it calls for. The higher the degree of autonomy sought after, the harder the struggle. It is therefore understandable that people tend to opt for prepacked projects, which could be likened to new conventions or even new forms of servitude (meaning the dependence of one person on another or on a system). Some of these are expressions of the great neoliberal and neo-authoritarian projects now proposed as economic and cultural models to which we should adjust as if there were no alternatives possible (even though the social and environmental catastrophe to which they are leading us is increasingly evident). These models include numerous ways of being and doing things that constitute the current supermarket offer of prepackaged identities. Its shelves contain a multifarious array: from successful professional to religious fundamentalist, from nostalgic hankerer after bygone communities to inhabitant of virtual networks.

These ways of being and doing things may be seen as pseudo-traditions since, in many ways, they appear to resemble what happened in traditional societies (they too offered/imposed a series of conventions that led to largely prepackaged life stories). However, there are some fundamental differences between the old traditions and the new pseudo-traditions. Unlike the old ways of doing things, the new ones—which we can also call disposable traditions—are adopted by choice (even though it may often feel like a forced choice, there are always other feasible options); they are not shared by the entire local society (since various possibilities are available contemporarily in the same sociocultural context, they produce social rifts); and they are the outcome of someone's project (recognizable in its motivations and in the means used to put it into effect, whereas those of the past seemed to be almost natural). At the same time, however, I do not believe that these new traditions can be relegated to the rank of superficial fads: when people adopt them they may profoundly modify their way of life and in some cases follow them to extreme, even tragic, consequences.

It follows that this magma of disposable traditions interweaving and mingling in our contemporary, fluid society suggests ways of escaping the complexity of reality and distracts from the possibility of thinking and developing highly autonomous projects. How can we counteract this tendency? What can we do to prevent the design resources, released by the disappearance of solid-world traditions, falling into the new traps of the fluid world? How can we help them develop their own autonomy and trigger collective learning processes?

Clearly, there are no easy answers to these questions. However, as discussed above, despite all the difficulties, I believe that some positive replies are possible. I think the design capabilities widely neglected in traditional societies, and that now tend to be channeled into new pseudo-traditions, can be used better. To find out how, we need to start by looking more closely at the actors on the field, their motivations, and the way they seek well-being and conceive their own life projects.

Exploring

Capabilities, tools, and results. One of the Lao Tzu's most famous quotes says: "Give a man a fish and you feed him for a day. Teach a man to fish and you feed him for a lifetime." About 2500 years ago, the question of relationship between autonomy and well-being had already been posed and had found an answer that is as relevant today as it was then: for lasting well-being, people must have the possibility of tackling their own problems through their own efforts. However, to do this they must have adequate knowledge and tools available. Today, possibly the most important of these tools is design capability.

To discuss this, we shall leap forward nearly 2500 years to the line of thinking started by Amartya Sen and Martha Nussbaum. In the 1990s, these writers laid the basis for an approach to the issue of well-being, and thus for the quest for happiness, which is close to the teaching of Lao Tzu. Instead of seeing people as carriers of needs to be satisfied (and therefore considering their well-being as a basket of products that should respond to their needs), Sen and Nussbaum suggested seeing them as actors endowed with capabilities that enable them to act and achieve results, such as "being fed, housed and adequately clothed ... being able to circulate freely, meet friends and have relationships with them, being able to appear in public without feeling ashamed, being able to communicate and participate, being able to follow one's own creative interests, and so on."[9] So, adopting this approach, a person is described as an active subject capable of seeking well-being by setting his own

---

[9] Amartya Sen and Martha Nussbaum (eds.), *The Quality of Life* (New York: Oxford University Press, 1993), Introduction.
The change of point of view proposed by Sen and Nussbaum has influenced numerous researchers in various disciplines. For design experts, it entails a radical change not only in the way of looking at potential users but also in the way of imagining one's own role: a shift from identifying problems

capabilities in motion. In other words, by looking at things in this way people are seen not only as carriers of needs but *also* of capabilities. Thus, they are not only part of the problems they find themselves facing but also actors in their solution.

Another interesting aspect of this interpretative model, for our discussion here, is that it allows us to talk about well-being (whether individual or social), shifting our focus from the availability of material goods to what they enable us to achieve. In particular, it allows us to talk about what can be achieved in terms of freedom: "freedom from" (from hunger, climatic adversities, uncertainty, solitude) and "freedom to" (to choose where to be and who with, what to do in terms of work, and how much to work, what ideas to present to the world and what to look like …). Put in the language of this book, this means that people's well-being is based on their design capability—on their freedom to design how to live—and to live a life that they themselves have, at least in part, designed autonomously.

To conclude this initial series of considerations, we can return to the protagonist of our story and say that his possibility of designing projects, and the quality of those projects, will depend on the design capability that he has been able to muster and cultivate (meaning his critical sense, his skills and abilities, his creativity, and his inclination to be active and to collaborate with others). However, this obviously also depends on the environment he is living in and in which he finds himself operating: an environment that may be more or less favorable to his using his own personal capabilities and to allowing their application to achieve positive results.

To understand a little better how the relationship between design capabilities and context could work out, we need to look more carefully at what designing actually means with reference to life projects. This also means focusing on the idea

---

and proposing solutions to identifying not only the problems but also, and above all, the capabilities and latent resources and developing systems able to promote and support them.

of life project that our protagonist has in mind and is seeking, more or less successfully, to apply.

Life projects as bricolage. A life project can be seen as a sequence of conversations and actions intended to achieve results pertaining to one's own life or part of it. This entails weighing up one's own personal resources and the context characteristics, focusing on a feasible vision of what one would like to achieve, and having the relational system and necessary tools at one's disposal.

In theory, things should go as follows: the protagonist of our story should outline a vision in the long term (the widest vision of what he would like to be and do) and organize himself to achieve it, deciding on the details as need arises day by day. In practice, however, what we actually see and live is a totally different situation: we are very often forced to rough out daily plans even when there is no long-term project or only a very vague one. It is then very often the experiences deriving from these explorative, contingency plans that lead us to construct our vision of the world, our expectations, and therefore our long-term projects. In other words, it is the projects for everyday life that constitute the building bricks for the overall life project. So, even though I shall continue to use the term "life project" for the sake of convenience, from now onward, I shall really be referring to partial projects, which focus on various aspects, problems, and moments. By interweaving with others, these will then give rise to overall life projects. To do all this, people adapt what they find along the way, reinterpreting it, and modifying its meaning, its use, and sometimes its actual physical constitution. In other words, they behave like *bricoleurs*.

The French anthropologist Claude Lévi-Strauss, who first introduced the figure of a *bricoleur*, with the meaning used here, compared it to that of an engineer.[10] Lévi-Strauss

---

[10] Claude Lévi-Strauss, *La Pensée sauvage* (Paris, 1962). English translation as *The Savage Mind* (Chicago, 1966). A *bricoleur* is a "Jack of all trades" or a kind of professional do-it-yourself person (Levi-Strauss, 1966), 17.

identified the engineer as someone who designs starting with a precise objective and then goes on to determine the means of achieving it. The *bricoleur*, on the other hand, sets himself an objective that he keeps open and uses the objects he finds to determine how to achieve it (and therefore also its final shape and form). So, the *bricoleur* also operates intentionally and therefore designs. But, unlike the engineer, he approximates his results by reassembling preexistent objects, which he identifies, decontextualizes, and reinterprets modifying their meaning and some of the details. This operation of decontextualization and reinterpretation is basic to his designing activity and is applied at all scales: from using old tire rubber to make shoe soles to transforming an old bus into a house. I believe that this design approach is the most applicable for operating in a world where we have to accept the complexity, whether we like it or not.

Underlying the way of acting that Lévi-Strauss attributes to the engineer is a simple world, or one reducible to simplicity (the world seen from a reductionist, mechanistic standpoint), in which the designer is imagined to know everything, control everything, and thus bend reality at his will. This idea of a designer, which we can call demiurgic, prevailed in the last century and is still widespread today, even though its inefficacy has long been evident. On the contrary, the *bricoleur* model and the dialogical attitude toward reality that underlies it are emerging precisely because they are proving more appropriate for navigating in complexity. The result is that, contrary to what modern thinking had imagined, bricolage is not a special case of design—a sort of lesser design—and the truth is quite the opposite: it is the engineer, in the stereotype used here, that represents the unusual way of proceeding, usable only in simple cases where it may really be supposed that all the information is available and the best way to act may be deduced from it.

Thus the designer-*bricoleur* proceeds through a series of findings, or rather, by working to make them happen: objects (products, services, procedures, and ideas) that appear to be potentially useful and with which he can create his storehouse.

On the other hand, since the objects in his storehouse are shaped according to their previous function, on meeting them, the designer-*bricoleur* recognizes a new strong functional and expressive potential, decides to give them a special role, and thus changes his final objective. Or alternatively, he might go down a completely different road. In other words, the project, like bricolage, is a continuous dialogue between the designer and the objects he finds. For this reason we can call it a *dialogical project*, capable of listening to the situation attentively and, if the case dictates, re-orientate his own pathway.

I think that it is precisely this dialogical nature that makes the reference to a *bricoleur* particularly useful when the project we are talking about is a life project. It allows us to avoid the paralyzing divide between power delirium and passivity: between denying reality, in seeking to appear as a demiurgic designer (with all the probable consequent frustrations), and tamely accepting it, adapting oneself to what appears to be its unalterable rules. Instead, the approach proposed here entails recognizing and accepting the complexity of the world, tackling it with a combination of intentionality and ability to recognize not only its limits and constraints but also the opportunities it offers. It encourages us to see things existent as things that can be transformed, and that the first step to take is to look at them in a different way, giving them new sense and new functionality.

An able *bricoleur* knows how to design through listening to things and to people, recognizing what he can contribute to the pathway being followed. What does he need in order to do so? First of all he needs a well-stocked "storehouse" of potentially useful items. For life projects, this storehouse contains the wealth and variety of what can be found in the socio-technical, cultural, and political ecosystem of which he is a part: the products, services, and infrastructures, and also the ideas, programs, ways of doing things, and formally defined methodologies. Then he needs internal resources: knowledge and values according to which to formulate and evaluate his project and the results deriving from it.

We shall continue from this last point. The switch from conventional mode (conforming to traditions and doing what has always been done) to design mode (making autonomous choices) entails extending our individual responsibility: designing always means making value choices, even when we are not aware of it, and thus we make *ethical* choices if by this adjective we mean choosing to evaluate according to the criterion of distinction between good and bad. This is not easy: How can we—in our everyday lives, in every design choice we make, alone and without the help of conventions—distinguish between good and bad? Obviously, there are no simple answers to this question. However, the image of designer as a *bricoleur* may help us.

Complexity and individual responsibility. The cultural background of the design approach I am now advocating is the acceptance, *and positive evaluation*, of complexity. This means not only accepting that every result of human activity should be considered provisional and reversible, and that our actions on the world will always have unpredictable implications (so we will never know, a priori, what the actual result will be in the long term or the full extent of their impact). It also means accepting that there is always a two-way tie between the person designing and the result of his project. This means that the designer is never external to the system on which he acts, or in short, that the design designs its designer.[11] In my view, being aware of this, knowing that in any case we cannot know everything and have the power to do everything, should reduce the risk of performance stress (when faced with the responsibility of designing a project) and make our designing activities more human: being able to imagine and act but at the same time being aware of the human limits to understanding our world. We are small creatures in a large, complex world.

---

[11] Anne-MarieWillis, *Ontological Design—Laying the Ground*, Design Philosophy Papers Collection Three (https://www.academia.edu/888457/Ontological_designing).

However, we can do something and take the responsibility for our choices. Let's take a closer look.

Reading the world as an irreducibly complex reality helps us redefine our role in it as human beings. If this is the way things are, if even the construction of the world we live in is a complex phenomenon, we can play a role that is significant but not determining. In other words, in complexity, every subjectivity has a weight and therefore a responsibility, but no subjectivity is able to dominate the entire system. It follows that if everyone has responsibility, no one has all the responsibility.

In my opinion this statement is significant, but it may be misunderstood. By it I mean that when dealing with complex problems, saying that the person operating is entirely responsible for what he does is theoretically unsustainable: by their very nature, complex systems do not have a viewpoint from which one can glean all the information and thus from which one can take all the responsibility. However, whoever acts in this complexity can, and indeed must, be ethically sensitive to the context (we can be "responsive," as Adam Thorpe and Lorraine Gamman wrote[12]). He must assume responsibility for everything he can see and do from his point of observation and action on the world, trusting that others will do the same from their points of observation and action. Ultimately, in complex systems the responsibility cannot but be the result of a collective intelligence. Of course, the context in which to apply this capacity to respond ethically extends to everything we can see and do from the point we are in. This goes far beyond what we should do according to the role we cover in the organizations we belong to. In other words, the cook in a death camp has a responsibility for what happens there. Although his task is only to cook, he has all the information necessary to recognize where he is and what is happening there.

---

[12] Adam Thorpe and Lorraine Gamman, "Design with Society: Why Socially Responsive Design Is Good Enough," *CoDesign: International Journal of CoCreation in Design and the Arts* 7, no. 3–4 (2011), 217–230.

This is not merely a theoretical observation. I think it also has an important operative implication. Attributing to a person who does things all the responsibility for the results of his actions (if taken seriously) is inevitably paralyzing. Or alternatively, it may lead to indifference: if we can't take all that responsibility, we might as well not take any. On the other hand, assuming an ethically responsive attitude means being able to read one's context, recognize one's own possibilities for action (including what is beyond one's formally recognized role at that moment), and assume complete responsibility for them.

Exploring and transforming the field of possibility. Every project should be seen as an exploration of the field of possibility (to be precise, on the basis of what I have just written, we should say, an exploration of what is just, fair, and possible. So, from here on, we shall assume that, in the choices we will be dealing with, the limits of possibility are also defined by what is ethically acceptable—by which I mean that it is considered not possible to do something that is not just and fair).

This is an exploration in the true sense of the word because, although it is certain that this field has its limits, it can never be fully known: like every aspect of reality, it too has a complex nature and is intrinsically unknowable. Using the metaphor of the *bricoleur* again, we can say that the field of possibility is limited by the nature and dimensions of the potentially usable items available, but its full extent cannot be known because the designer cannot be sure that his storehouse contains all the items that, in theory, could be used; that he would not be able to find others if he were to look more carefully; and that tomorrow he would not be able to imagine new uses for those that he already has.

In other words, the field of possibility is everything that the nature, culture, economy, and technology of a given society allow to be done in a given place and time. It includes the spaces of freedom within which each subject can theoretically move. In short, the field of possibility is everything that it is not impossible to do, whereas the field of action is that part of the theoretically possible that a person thinks he can put into practice using his own personal resources. It therefore consists of the spaces of freedom that each subject thinks he can have.

For this reason, since a life project emerges out of the choices that a person makes within what he sees as his field of action, it may be possible for him to increase his range of feasible options in two complementary ways. The first consists in extending his field of action by improving his personal resources (capabilities, skills, interests, and creativity) and thus using a larger area of the field of theoretical possibility. The second consists in widening his field of possibility by reducing the technical, regulatory, financial, and cultural limits of the system with which subjects interact. Normally, it is assumed that the only road accessible from the bottom, meaning from the position of our protagonist, is the former, whereas the latter, which entails changing limits of the system, calls for external intervention from above. At a first glance, this may appear to be true. However, things may go differently: the field of possibility can also be forced, meaning extended from the inside and from below if and when our protagonist, like an able *bricoleur*, reinterprets the meaning of some of the elements in the local system in an original way or modifies them to fit his own objectives.

When this happens, we can talk about an autonomous project, in the sense that it does not accept the field of possibility available at a particular time and place as if it were inevitable but works to modify it. Obviously, how and to what extent these actions, which are intended to change the field of possibility from the inside and from the bottom upward, may be effective depend on many factors. For now we shall just say that the more our protagonist manages to collaborate with others, the greater his possibility of success.

Collaborating

Collaborative projects and autonomy. Until now, when talking about the social dimension of life projects, I have been referring to activities supported by a social network but that aim to achieve a result that is substantially individual. Now I would like to focus on cases in which a person's life project interweaves with others leading to collaborative activity and shared results.

Consider, for example, that our protagonist chooses to participate in a cohousing project, or is a plant enthusiast and decides to take part in looking after a neighborhood garden, or that he suffers from diabetes and joins a mutual-help group for people affected by the same illness. In each of these cases, those involved in the activity leave their individual role (that of consumer, client, or user) to become proactive collaborators in solving the problems that they find themselves facing. In so doing, their life projects converge and intertwine around an issue of shared interest, creating a collaborative activity.[13] This means an activity in which each of the participants achieves a result by working with others that he would not have been able to achieve alone: a result that can only be achieved if a similar result is achieved by the other participants in the initiative at the same time.

Returning to the examples mentioned above, we can see that by living collaboratively it is possible to create self-managed nurseries, services for the elderly, purchasing groups, and neighborhood sport and recreational activities that would otherwise have been unthinkable. Similarly, by working together in a neighborhood garden, plant enthusiasts can enjoy more than just a pot on the balcony, or people suffering from the same illness may be able to find better help and support for everyday problems together than can be provided by the normal health service. So, generalizing, we can say that by adopting a collaborative approach, our protagonist can achieve better results. This is because collaboration modifies the system in which it operates and not only extends its

---

[13] Richard Sennet, *Together: The Ritual, Pleasure, and Politics of Cooperation* (New Haven: Yale University Press, 2012).

field of action but also its field of possibilities. However, it goes without saying that to imagine and set up one's own collaborative life project, it is necessary to distance oneself from the processes of exasperated individualization that still dominate contemporary society, thus creating, consciously or unconsciously, a local discontinuity at cultural level. It follows that as well as demonstrating the force of collaboration and the possibility it offers for solving otherwise difficult problems, such collaborative projects also express a higher degree of autonomy. Indeed, whereas individual life projects and the practical procedures they entail struggle to escape from the constraints of the great dominant projects (those that in the name of individual freedom tend to cage everyone into an everyday life imposed by others and an individualism as extreme as it is impotent), collaborative projects are able to do so and thus become more autonomous. Ultimately, it appears that the greatest autonomy, in terms of individual projects, is achieved when one agrees to join forces with others and work together. The result is a strong correlation between autonomy and collaboration: when one grows so does the other, and vice versa.

Collaborative living, as an example. To talk about life projects I have considered two extremes, which can be seen as polarities: projects that are necessarily entirely individual and projects that are expressly collaborative (as in the examples of social innovation mentioned in the previous paragraph). However, a closer look shows us that since all human actions are immersed in a network of interactions and conversations, there will always be a certain degree of collaboration. So, between the two poles, individual projects and expressly collaborative ones, there is a continuum of situations that entail various degrees of engagement for the actors involved. It follows that what I say about expressly collaborative projects will also be true, though to a lesser degree, for projects where the level of collaboration is lower. To argue my point, I will refer to life projects connected with ways of living and, in particular, those concerned with *collaborative living*.

The expression "collaborative living" refers to a way of living home, neighborhood, and city that includes shared spaces and services in a general framework of self-organization, mutual help, friendship, and neighborliness. The idea may seem absolutely obvious: in all housing cultures, in every period of history, human beings have created ways of living together, sharing and collaborating. Consequently, it should not be necessary to call on any special kind of designing capability. However, if this idea is proposed today as ground for social innovation, and is fruit of special design capabilities, it is because somewhere along the line something has happened that has removed the obviousness of collaboration from contemporary society. Nowadays, a mixture of ideas and issues concerning well-being (quest for individual freedom and privacy), demographic conditions (crisis of the family, aging population), working mode (job insecurity and unemployment), perception of time (there never seems enough), and a sense of insecurity (which leads to segregation for fear of others) tends to produce ways of living characterized by growing isolation and the loss of ability to collaborate. The result is that the dominant tendency is toward solitary, technologically assisted living: an isolated life, supported by virtual social services and networks. On the other hand, this isolated life assisted by technological gadgets is unable to respond to many of people's practical, psychological, and cultural needs. In addition, it does not create the cohesion necessary to prevent isolated people being overcome by fear in the face of the unknown factors and disasters of present times.

For this reason, and fortunately, this solitary living is being called to question by radically different ways of doing things—ways of acting that lead to a rediscovery of the value of collaboration and to finding ways of putting it into practice. These activities are the ground from which innovative practices of collaborative living have emerged, those that here we are considering for what, to all intents and purposes, they are: the result of applying remarkable designing capabilities.

The history of collaborative living, in the sense I am using it here, began with the ideas and practices emerging in Europe and the United States at the end of the last century. Specifying this starting point is important in order to signal its differences from the various forms of communal living that have existed for centuries in all premodern societies (where the nature and shape of collaboration were determined by tradition and by its conventions). The collaborative living we are talking about here, on the other hand, is born from choice and nurtured with constant care for its proper functioning. However, the history of collaborative living is also different from those of other ways of living together, of sharing and of collaborating, such as the American hippy communes of the sixties or the Israelian kibbutz. Indeed, quite apart from certain superficial similarities, hippy communes and kibbutz were both, in different ways, forms of cohabitation built on strong ideologies. They were founded on the ethical and political tenet that it was right to live together, sharing and collaborating. Having made this fundamental choice, the life project that led to these practices was the necessary consequence.

The collaborative living we talk about today is not like this. Nowadays, the starting point is a practical agreement within the general framework of an idea, open and intentionally left vague, of neighborliness and collaboration: a group of individuals and families discuss how to live better sharing certain services and establishing good mutual relationships. They do so because, in some way, they like the idea of living near each other and sharing something, but the crucial point is what they actually choose to do together, in practical terms, and how to do it. The whole proposal rests on this point and from here derives the social and cultural sense of what they are doing.

In other words, whereas both kibbutz and communes were emblematic cases in different contexts of life projects motivated by strong ideologies (and which produced communities that were also based on shared strong ideological convictions), collaborative living appeared right from the start as an unprecedented way of designing one's own life that has produced equally unprecedented social forms: the substantially post-ideological communities of the twenty-first century, meaning spaces of opportunity for pragmatic conversations about what we can and would like to do together.

To discuss this question further, I shall refer to a design research program developed by the DESIS Lab at the Politecnico di Milano, in collaboration with various partners, started over ten years ago, and that is still going ahead in different forms, along different lines of action and with diverse social actors as protagonists.[14] The first stage of this program concentrated on cohousing: groups of families who decide autonomously to live near each other, sharing spaces and services, and autonomously deciding the rules for their cohabitation and their relationship with the local neighborhood and the city as a whole.

Communities of interest and communities of purpose. When the program started in 2006, the idea of cohousing had been around for some time in Europe and the rest of the world. So, the first move was to analyze existing cases in depth so as to understand better what they were really like: the results they had achieved and the problems they faced. It emerged that despite strong motivation and widespread interest in the idea, its actual realization had met with considerable difficulty (with the result that the number of examples actually operating was low). In other words, people expressed an idea that they would have liked to develop into a project, but for various reasons, this did not happen.

Therefore, the program set itself the task of creating an enabling ecosystem to facilitate the realization of these

---

[14] The Programma Abitare Collaborativo was promoted by the Politecnico di Milano DESIS Lab, starting in 2006. The initial project, developed in collaboration with a social enterprise, has produced various cohousing initiatives in Milan and has provided a model for other similar activities in Italy. This initial activity spawned further lines of work that have led to various research and teaching activities and the start of other social enterprises dedicated to the theme of collaborative living.

hypothetical projects. The aim was to support and develop people's design capability and reduce the obstacles that they would otherwise have come up against. To do this, the potential demand was analyzed, together with the reasons why it was so difficult to transform plan into action. From this, and assuming the position of the people directly concerned (the future cohousers), three main difficulties were identified: first, getting in contact with other people interested in the project and able to start at the same time; second, finding a suitable area of land for building, or a suitable building for renovation, and negotiating bureaucratic and financial difficulties associated with their purchase; third, collaboratively designing the shared spaces and the activities necessary for their collaborative management. Confronted with these difficulties, a series of initiatives were set up to overcome them.

The first was the creation of a wide *community of interest:* a light community, supported by a digital platform and a team of experts from the housing market. The platform enabled people interested in the project to make contact with each other, and the housing experts drew everybody's attention to available buildings or land areas potentially suitable for a cohousing project. This community gathered together several thousand people and has had an almost exclusively digital life. I say almost exclusively digital because although its daily functioning was online, some offline encounters were also proposed for cultural and community-building purposes.

In relation to this community, we should note that the purpose-designed digital platform was essential for various reasons. The first and most fundamental is that the peculiarities of this tool enabled the community to gather a number of potentially interested people who would never have been reached without it. In other words, this is a case of a digital tool that was not merely a support for a community that could have existed without it; rather, it was the very precondition for the community to exist. A second more evident reason is that this platform performed the role of an organizational tool, coordinating activities. Last but not least, it also worked as a communication tool: spreading the idea of cohousing toward a much wider public than that already informed, producing a positive image of this way of living, and providing examples with which those interested could match themselves and compare their own personal ideas on the theme.

From this first great community, other smaller ones were born, each of them focusing on a particular, possible building or building area. These were *communities of purpose* oriented toward creating one specific cohousing initiative. The process consisted of three stages and three different community conformations. In the first, each community was a relatively large group of potential cohousers. Its purpose was to verify the effective interest of the participants and share the first ideas about how they would like to proceed. In the second stage, the group consolidated and decided the spaces to share and the activities to carry out collaboratively. Each community also created a formal association, deciding its statute and rules for good neighborly relations. Finally, in the third stage the community, now formally an association, declared its autonomy from the external team and took over the management and coordination of everyday activities. The activities in the three stages mainly took place offline, but with the support of a dedicated digital platform that enabled online activities. The team of experts that promoted and supported the initiative, and to all intents and purposes operated as part of the community, also changed with time, including different expertise according to the various stages of the project (in particular, experts in communication, new media, interior architecture and services, all with cross-disciplinary experience in codesigning).

Enabling ecosystems and designing coalitions. As already stated in the previous chapter, in the case described the community of interest and those of purpose played complementary roles: the first (community of interest) without the second (communities of purpose) would have risked getting bogged down in theory and principles, unable to impact on practice. Vice versa, the communities of purpose without reference to a community of interest in which to accumulate experiences and further reflections would have risked not having the critical and cultural background necessary to avoid setting off along impracticable paths or to avoid losing the ethical, social, and environmental values from which the original idea had emerged, as they evolved.

It is therefore these actions together that produce "assisted cohousing," meaning a type of cohousing where, thanks to an *enabling ecosystem* (i.e., various communities, support teams of experts, digital platforms, codesign tools, and service coproduction), the individual life projects of the various participants can develop more easily and interweave together, producing forms of collaboration that would otherwise have been difficult to create.

Observing how things actually go in practice in such cases, an issue arises that is crucial for us: the relationship between open, light communities of residents and more solid groups that operate within them as project-designing and project-management teams. In our cohousing example, we can see how its characterizing communities were born and now live, thanks to the activism of some of the community members. These people, alone or in collaboration with experts, operate as designers, managers, and often producers of the activities that, with time, lead to the building, management, and regeneration of the communities they are part of. It is important to note that the groups that these proactive people form are not fixed and their borders are permeable. By this, I mean that the people who make up these groups change as time passes. There is no clear divide between those who are proactive, and therefore part of the designing coalition, and those who are not. In other words, they are a direct, dynamic expression of the community and its way of life and not a consolidated power group. It is equally important to note that in this group there may also be various people who play an expert role. The number and nature of these experts may vary from case to case and from moment to moment (and so it was in our example of cohousing).

These observations may be generalized. The case of cohousing confirms what we have already said (see Chapter 1): contemporary communities are the result of interweaving conversations linked in a light and fluid way to common themes and issues; to be lasting, however, these communities must include designing coalitions,[15] in the sense of groups that vary with time, of people from within or from outside the community. These people are often motivated to act by different factors but have converging ideas about the results to achieve, and together they have the skills and abilities needed to put into practice what they have decided to do. Being able to form these coalitions and keep them active, while keeping their relationship with the rest of the group open and dynamic, is crucial to the positive functioning of every collaborative activity, and thus of every community to which it refers.

To conclude, a good enabling system is one that makes it possible for various people to participate in collaborative activities and the life of a community—to do so in different ways and with varying degrees of commitment and responsibility. Some may be *active* in the activities that the community proposes; others may be *proactive* and *creative* in the definition of the activities themselves (and it is these that keep the community itself active). By allowing everybody to find their own way of participating, this enabling ecosystem brings out, catalyzes, and systemizes the resources potentially available. To do so, however, it must not only offer people the possibility of getting involved in the ways and times possible for them. It must also articulate a cultural proposal in such a way as to align it with their diverse motivations and/or trigger new ones.

---

[15] The expression "designing coalition," as it is used here, also includes the evolution of the initial, strictly designing coalition toward a coalition that operates in the production and management stage of an initiative (if it is legitimate to extend this expression to these stages, it is because, as we have seen, in a fluid world, these stages too are characterized by a considerable designing component).

Collaboration and relational values. As mentioned earlier, interest for the practical results obtainable is not the only reason that leads our protagonist and others like him to embark on life projects based on collaborative practices. Other good reasons stem from a recognition of value in the friendship, trust, and empathy that projects of this type tend to produce, precisely because they are collaborative. Friendship, trust, and empathy are *relational values*:[16] intangibles that meet human needs as important as those satisfied by tangible goods. Let's look more closely at how this happens and the problems it may entail.

Experience tells us that relational values emerge when encounters take place in which we share common objectives and work together to achieve them. For this reason, life projects that are truly collaborative *also* produce this kind of value. On the other hand, it has to be said that collaboration and the relational values that derive from it do not come free. Their most evident cost is the time and attention called for to build the group. In addition, collaborating entails negotiating with others how and when to do something together, and this too may be lived as a cost in terms of constraints on individual freedom (or one's perception of this). Lastly, collaboration requires openness and willingness toward others, which on the one hand is what gives these interactions a more human character, but on the other—as discussed in the previous chapter—is what makes them emotionally demanding and because of this not always easily accessible.[17] It follows that motivation to collaborate is hampered by the perceived cost in terms of time, attention, and constraints to personal, individual

---

[16] Pierpaolo Donati, *Teoria relazionale della società* (Milano: Franco Angeli, 1991); P. L. Sacco and Stefano Zamagni, *Civil Economy, Cultural Evolution and Participatory Development: A Theoretical Enquiry* (Bologna: Università di Bologna, 1998).

[17] Carla Cipolla, "*Designing for Interpersonal Relational Qualities in Services*," doctoral thesis, Politecnico di Milano, 2007; see also Carla Cipolla and Ezio Manzini, "Relational Services," *Knowledge, Technology and Policy* 22 (2009), 45–50.

freedom. How to balance accessibility and relational quality in each case is, in my opinion, the main design problem in developing every collaborative social form.

This example of assisted cohousing clearly indicates how this issue can be tackled. The first instances of cohousing resulted from the life projects of highly motivated people who were prepared to shoulder the not insignificant difficulties of operating in environments that were relatively hostile. Therefore, such projects were accessible only to a restricted group of particularly dedicated people. Assisted cohousing, however, by creating enabling ecosystems, has opened the project to a wider group of people (to people with less time and energy available), and it has done so by trying to maintain and regenerate the original values. The same is true for subsequent experiences, when the idea of assisted cohousing was extended to collaborative living in various social housing initiatives.[18] In these cases, too, the course of action was to increase accessibility while maintaining the production of relational values and to offer individual life projects the possibility of intermingling with collective initiatives, balancing these two contrasting aspects: accessibility, and thus a more efficient use of resources, and the relational quality between participants.

I shall return to this in the following chapter. For the moment, it is enough to say that in the evolutionary trajectory of a collaborative solution, it is right and important to make it more accessible—thus lighter in terms of the time, energy, and attention called for; less rigid in the time constraints it imposes; and more capable of modulating the relational intensity of the interactions on which it is based. However, when moving in

---

[18] The experience of assisted cohousing has been taken up and developed by the Fondazione Housing Sociale (FHS), an institution dedicated to the development of social housing in Italy, which has included the concept of collaborative housing in its housing schemes with a positive outcome. It has used and further developed various ideas and design tools produced in previous cohousing experiences. Giordana Ferri (ed.), *Starting-up Communities. Un design-kit per l'abitare collaborativo* (Milano: Bruno Mondadori, 2016).

this direction, we must make sure that all this does not lead to the loss of its initial collaborative character, to the end of its ability to *also* produce relational values. On the contrary, we can say that the production of these relational values is to be seen as the best indicator of the quality of a successful collaborative solution at the various stages of its evolution toward maturity.

Visions of sustainable everyday life. In addition to everything noted so far, collaborative projects and their activities also produce discontinuities on a wider political and cultural level. Indeed, the results they lead to outline visions of a different world from that depicted in dominant thinking. Using our previous examples, we can observe that each of them has a high degree of autonomy in redefining the currently prevailing sense system and creating new scenarios. Because of this, anyone choosing to participate in a cohousing endeavor indicates a tangible alternative way of living. Similarly, anyone who takes care of a neighborhood garden demonstrates another way of thinking and managing a city. Anyone organizing a mutual-help group introduces a new perspective on the issue of care. Ultimately, anyone conceiving and developing a collaborative life project not only achieves positive results for himself and for the community he is part of but also participates in the production of a wider vision: that of a new civilization based on sustainable ways of being and doing things.

All this clearly has a political significance for what, in the next chapter, we shall call politics of everyday life. Politics that by themselves are certainly not enough to move the world out of the catastrophic trajectory along which it is moving but which may very well be the precondition for this to happen.

3

Politics of Everyday Life: Design Activism and Transformative Normality

When we came to live here, over twenty years ago, local fruit and vegetables were a rarity. Unless there was an elderly person in the family who still kept a vegetable garden, the fruit and vegetables available came from who knows where, just as in the city. Yet we were in the country, in an area with a great agricultural tradition. In previous years, with a few precious exceptions, an idea of food production and consumption that had lost all connection with the place and with the natural cycle of the seasons had pervaded this agricultural area.

Twenty years later, in the same place, it is no longer so difficult to find local fruit and vegetables: the Covered Farmers' Market[1] is open every day, stocked and run by local farmers (including seventy farming businesses and small agri-food producers). The quality is good and the price is fair. Access is simple: producing, selling, and buying these products has become quite normal.

---

[1] Il Mercato Coperto degli Agricoltori, Montevarchi (AR) (https://www.facebook.com/ilmercatalemontevarchi/)

It seems to me that this normality has great *political* value if by this adjective we denote something that impacts on policy: on the shape of socio-technical systems and the balance of power within them. Buying and selling in this market means keeping active from day to day a way of producing and consuming that counteracts the prevailing one: a collaborative way of doing things that expresses a high degree of autonomy (in the sense given in the previous chapter) and a way of conceiving the relationship between production and food consumption, and between local area and community, that brings back an apparently long-forgotten idea of locality—one that clashes with the dominant logic of large-scale, mass-market, industrial agriculture. Nowadays, the clash between ways of thinking and doing things no longer seems so evident in this local area because, as previously mentioned, this localized model is satisfactorily consolidated. However, it is a normality that is collaborating in a system change: a transformative normality, the existence of which modifies, even on a larger scale, the existing balance (in economic terms and in terms of power and knowledge).

The transformative normality we can see today is the result of a history of social and cultural activism. The events that led to the farmers' market in its current form began over ten years ago on the initiative of local farmers (the precious exceptions I was talking about), in collaboration with Slow Food and the Montevarchi town council. Thanks to their activism, it was possible to open the first prototype of a farmers' market. This took place one Sunday a month and as well as a market, it was also a festivity and a cultural event. It was also a strong political declaration in favor of production and consumption models opposed to what was currently in place, made by the promoters of the initiative and by those who took part in various other ways. It was this militant activity that catalyzed latent interests and, as far as food was concerned, gave visibility to a different way of thinking and doing things. On a practical plane, this series of market-events created the first direct contacts between local producers and purchasers (at that time still largely potential) and started to create the initial forms of demand and offer. Without this past of activism and creativity, the current transformative reality would not have been possible.

Continuing the story, we shall see that in order to arrive at the Covered Farmers' Market as it exists today, it was necessary to accomplish a delicate changeover: from the initial, heroic stage—when a group of enthusiasts, gifted with creativity, managerial skills, and practical sense, set up the first market prototypes—to the stage that gave the market continuity, which called for the gifts of realism and political sense. This change was necessary to transform the initial events into a stable reality, a market easily accessible to many on a daily basis.

Acting

Everyday life makes policies. This change from the nascent stage, of politics as activism, to that of daily life is a crucial moment, one in which many such initiatives have failed. The initial activists, the social heroes who imagine and create something radically new, often turn in on themselves and tend to block the initiative itself, effectively restricting access to the super-committed, initial small group (until even their energy and enthusiasm burn out). Or, on the contrary, the initiative may evolve toward mature solutions that, in the name of efficiency, completely lose the values from which they had started and, in the worst-case scenario, the ideas of service on which they are based evolve into new neoliberal models. Like other similar examples, the farmers' market we have seen shows us that a third way exists, somewhere between the closed minority group and the drift toward updated neoliberalism. So, it is a question of understanding how and when this happens— what choices need to be made and what everyday-life policies to be adopted. The Montevarchi Farmers' Market shows us that the promoters were able to follow a trajectory that led the original initiative to find a feasible balance between economic effectiveness and social and environmental values.

Obviously, as for all social forms, nobody can know how it will evolve as time goes on. However, we can certainly say that, at the moment, it has enabled small local farmers to exist, and many citizens to recognize and appreciate the quality of their production and its value for the local economy.

Therefore, this case tells us how people like the farmers and local citizens in Montevarchi can make choices in their everyday lives that not only influence their own lives but also, with their tangible example, impact on the socio-technical systems on which they are based and ultimately on the wider socioeconomic balance and cultural equilibrium. In addition, by cultivating and regenerating collaborative capability and production of commons, everyday actions can play a political role in the transition toward sustainability. Of course, they are not an organic political program and will never be able to constitute one—not only because the local and contingent way in which they emerge cannot be planned but also because by their very nature they are far distant from what we normally mean by "politics."

The everyday-life policies I have been talking about so far do not imply putting everyday actions at the service of politics: they are not propaganda, and they do not support any political party or movement. Rather, they are events that are capable of changing the state of things by their very existence, because they are tangible examples of ways of being and doing things that differ from, and often counteract, dominant ways. In their book *L'arte fuori di sé*, Andrea Balzola and Paolo Rosa say that "their art is not political, but is in itself policy, meaning it produces a project to reconfigure behaviour and collective sensitivity, autonomously from politics" (meaning the politics of political parties).[2] Balzola and Rosa say this about art, but I

---

[2] I like starting this chapter with this quote from Paolo Rosa. Paolo was a great artist and a friend who left us too soon. However, he had time to teach many people, and me in particular, some important things. Among these there is one that gives a sense frame to everything that I will try to argue in this chapter:

believe that the idea can be extended to the art of living, that is, to life in general and how merely the way we live has political implications. Ultimately, everyday actions are not political, but every action may in itself be policy—and a very meaningful one.

The world seen (and constructed) by those who live in it. The local and the everyday are the theater of life for human beings, but they are also the open construction site in which this theater is constantly rebuilt and adapted and sometimes radically transformed. Here, our protagonist enters the scene. He is collocated in a precise point of space and time, and from here he confronts life and its problems and makes his choices. His observation and action point on the world is his "local," meaning an environment that is defined not so much by its physical as by its operational dimensions. What is local is the world as it can be seen by an individual or a community. Thus, referring to what is local does not so much imply a dimensional limit, but rather a human limit: it means accepting that anything we think and do, we can inevitably only think or do from where we find ourselves. If traditionally we assume that local refers to a small physical space, it is because, from their point of view, individuals and communities in the past were not able to see far and similarly they could only act in proximity. Today things have changed, and this change is one of the many ways globalization can be described.

The sociologist Anthony Giddens wrote that globalization is "the intensification of worldwide social relations which link distant localities in such a way that local happenings are shaped by events occurring many miles away and vice versa."[3] What appears interesting to me in this definition is the opening: it does not introduce a specific field of activity or make any value

the things we do have, in themselves, a political sense. They may even have a revolutionary political sense. A. Balzola and P. Rosa, *L'arte fuori di sé* (Milano: Feltrinelli, 2012), p. 176.

[3] A. Giddens, *The Consequences of Modernity* (Cambridge: Polity, 1990), p. 64.

judgment. It introduces just one distinctive criterion: there is globalization if there is a dense, rapid, wide-ranging network of interactions, such that what happens in one place can be influenced by what happens in other places, independently of their geographic location. This is exactly what is happening today: the interaction network is so dense and the interactions so fast and wide-ranging that what is to us local, and the happenings we can generate here, is shaped by other events happening thousands of miles away, and vice versa. This augmented locality, this hyperlocal whose borders depend on the communication networks we are part of, is therefore the point from which our protagonist observes the world and acts on it.

So, let's go back to our protagonist and consider him in an everyday situation (one that is very common): like every morning, he is trapped in his car, in the middle of the urban traffic, on his way to work. At this moment his environment is determined by many widely differing systems: natural systems, such as the topography and climate of the place (which trap the exhaust fumes from the vehicles, polluting the air around), or the long-term artificial ones that have shaped the city, its activities, and its road system in a certain way (so that his home is a long way from his office and he has to commute for some distance every day). Then there are those short-term artificial ones: such as the way working hours are organized (making everyone travel to work at the same time); transport policies (that privilege private vehicles over public transport); the car industries (that have produced the very car our protagonist is driving); the communication systems that broadcast music and news over the radio, and texts, emails, and phone calls (that keep him occupied or distract him); and so forth.

These systems together, and each of them separately, can be considered according to their nature and their structure. To do so we need to imagine we are looking down on them from above, as a whole. This is the observation point of experts. For those in the car, what they see is very different: all these systems merge together, perceived synthetically as well-being;

or alternatively, and I think at the moment, in that environment this is more probable, as discomfort.

Supposing that, as I suspect, discomfort is prevailing, there is a choice to make: our protagonist can trust to his capacity to adapt and accept things as they are (we know that human beings are able to adapt to different environments) or refuse to. In the second case, he must apply his other capability, his designing capability, and imagine an action strategy to get out of the condition he is in. Continuing along the road, our protagonist soon comes to another crossroads: he can focus on the problem and try to get someone else to solve it (e.g., he can vote for another political party), or he can take part in an environmental demonstration (to convince those in power to solve it), or again, he can try to solve it himself by individual action or in collaboration with others.

The first and second roads are those that we normally call politics: do something to get someone else to try and find the solution. Important as this is, and important as it would be to talk about it, I am not going to do so here, because it falls outside the aims of this book. Instead, here I am going to look into the third possibility, at what our protagonist may do, alone or in collaboration with others, to resolve the problem. How can I set everyday-life policies in action?

Change the world from where you are. The expression *everyday-life policy* indicates a sequence of actions that may influence the socio-technical systems (and therefore also the economic, political, and cultural ones) in which we operate and with which we come into contact: actions on the world, concerning everyday life, performed from where we are—from our own point of observation and action. In other words, an everyday-life policy is the systemic effect of a life project.

So, let's go back to our protagonist while, like every morning, he is in his car, stuck in the urban traffic, slowly trying to get to work. If he decides to do something himself to get out of this predicament, what could he actually do? Well, there is something, and he can do it by following various strategies. For example, he could buy whatever he needs to live better, relaxing, socializing, and working while he is in the car. Alternatively, if a public transport system exists and is efficient, he can choose to leave the car at home and go to work by bus or train. Or again, if age and distance allow it, he can buy a bike and use it for his day-to-day movements. Lastly, he could come to an agreement with others and use the same car (reducing stress and traveling in company), effectively joining or organizing a carpooling system. There are also other more radical strategies possible: if the type of activity he does is suitable, he can organize himself to work from home and reduce the need to face the traffic every day to go to the office. Alternatively, he could move house and go to live near the office, or he could stop working and change his whole way of life. However, for simplicity's sake, we shall stop at the first four possibilities, the ones that do not question his need to travel to work and back home every day. They correspond to different policies in the sense that they affect, in different ways, not only him but also the system with which he interacts.

The first strategy enables our protagonist to improve his environment without modifying it in depth. The underlying idea is: "Since I have to spend so much time in the car, let's see how I can make that time more useful and pleasant." This choice is the most coherent with the dominant cultural and behavioral framework (it is no coincidence that it is the most common strategy nowadays). We could call it the inertial choice: given a problem, we try to overcome the difficulty and discomfort it causes by finding technical solutions to minimize it.

The second strategy, using public transport, is certainly the most effective whenever feasible. It is also the simplest. Although it calls for a considerable behavioral change, leaving the car and taking public transport is a common way out and is generally socially acceptable. The problem with this choice is its rigidity: if public transport is there and works well, there are no problems. On the other hand, if there is no public transport or what exists is inefficient, it becomes an almost impossible option.

The third and fourth strategies call for a greater behavioral change: cycling to work entails changing one's habits and ideas of comfort and status (in the sense that pedaling to the office rather than using the car has to become socially acceptable to the person concerned), whereas deciding for the fourth strategy and opting for carpooling entail accepting the complications of agreeing routes and times with other people and building a relationship of mutual trust with them (who is this person getting in my car? Who is the person driving this car?). Moreover, carpooling produces new social forms: the group in a shared car is not a family or a group of friends; neither is it a taxi driver–client relationship. It is a new social form, the nature of which requires better understanding.

The four possibilities that I have just schematically outlined show how our protagonist himself could act to change his own environment. In our imaginary example, he was able to choose from four different options that were, in principle, equally feasible—something that is rarely possible. In any event, remaining within this theoretical example, in order to make his choice and put it into practice, our protagonist had to apply his design capability: recognize the availability of alternatives, understand their possibilities, and, having made his choice, put it into practice. From here, to continue the discussion on everyday-life policies, I would like to talk about the way in which the four strategies indicated, though motivated by personal choice and operating on the local environment, may also have an effect on a larger scale.

The systemic effects of everyday choices. By adopting the first strategy—improving the liveability of cars—one's freedom of choice is used to hollow out a niche of relative local well-being, accepting the nature of the context. By doing this (by considering the urban traffic situation to be inevitable) our protagonist fails to call the transport system into question, which not only remains unchanged but, given the reduced sensitivity toward the most pressing problems it is causing, tends to consolidate: there is less incentive for car drivers who phone, chat, and text in their air-conditioned, mobile lounge-offices to react to the absurdity of the traffic. Thus, they will be more willing to accept it because "at any rate, I'm not wasting time."

On the other hand, we know that the intelligence of a complex system can be measured by the feedback it receives, enabling it to sound out the general climate around it (with the problems that may arise there) and adapt itself accordingly. In this case, car drivers who experience traffic stress firsthand are the best sensors available to the urban system to register the inadequacies of its transport. For this reason, air-conditioning, music, and connectivity in the car reduce driver sensitivity and their inclination to react. In effect, this makes the overall system more "stupid." At the same time, a choice of this kind gives an indication and stimulus to the electronic and car industries, pushing them to look for solutions that meet the demand for "mobile comfort" better (even though, in this case, the mobility is relative given the persistent road blockages). The result is that the electronics and telecommunications sector as well as the car sector develops in this direction, consolidating an unsustainable evolutionary trajectory.

From all points of view, a connected individual, shut alone in his car and blocked in the traffic, is the emblematic representation of the absurdity, even before the environmental and social unsustainability, of the everyday life proposed to millions of people.

By contrast, choosing bus or train travel, where feasible, is also a clear indication to those who are in a position to decide at wider system level that public transport is important—that it should be supported and improved where necessary. Furthermore, since improving public transport requires large-scale system designing, what our protagonist can do (apart from using the existing system, if available) is to act on a political level in a traditional way (by voting or joining a political movement committed to this issue) and, where possible, take part in codesigning processes that aim to direct future developments of the transport system, putting to good purpose what he has learned as a user.

Now let's go on to the other two strategies for solving the problem, using a bike or carpooling: two options that in many places are considered to be local discontinuities (see Chapter 1). Though different, both of them question the still dominant equation: individual mobility = private car. This break with continuity at individual or small-group level, together with other similar discontinuities, could encourage the institutions in charge of traffic and urban planning to create new cycling paths or reserved lanes and parking for carpoolers; or as is already happening in some cities, it could induce them to redefine the entire plan for traffic circulation, fostering the use of bikes and alternative mobility in general, thus creating a system change at city level (Chapter 1).

In short, these local choices, and the local discontinuities they create, have a double effect: for those who take them up they are solutions to immediate problems, but they can also influence the socio-technical system they are applied to at a larger scale, orienting its evolution in a different direction from what had appeared dominant until then. Obviously, this large-scale effect is only a possibility. If our protagonist were the only person to choose to cycle, he would still find himself pedaling in the traffic in the future. Similarly, if the carpooling option were to remain a minority choice and no preferential lanes were to be designated, his shared car would still be blocked in the traffic jam with everybody else. Nevertheless, making choices like these means our protagonist is able to put into practice the possibility he has available to him in his everyday life to impact on systems, to make something happen that is meaningful not only to himself but also to the overall society. Thus, whether consciously or not, with his actions he is playing a designing and a political role in the future of society as a whole.

In the previous chapter, with reference to ways of proceeding like this one, I talked about autonomy. Now I shall add that this autonomy lies at the basis of everyday policies that are capable of changing the world. Not everybody, however, is of the same opinion. Everyday life and the choices made in it can also be read in a completely different way from what has been proposed so far.

Transgressing

Can we escape the control apparatus? The scenario outlined so far shows people who have the possibility of moving outside the system, rebelling against dominant ways of doing things and, consciously or not, take a political stance in their everyday lives, demonstrating a high degree of autonomy. Obviously, things can also be seen in another way, and before continuing we must take this into consideration. From this other point of view, which is the opposite of mine, society becomes an inescapable control system. In the past century, it was said that this control was carried out by a variety of institutions: family, factory, school, barracks, hospital, nursing home, or prison.[4] Undoubtedly, nowadays this way of seeing things also includes the even more ubiquitous control through digital media, the algorithms on which these are based, and the data processing that can be carried out.[5] For those who think this way, all resistance tactics, all the strategies I have indicated in the previous paragraph, come to the same thing: whatever you do, you cannot escape control by the system.

Actually, this vision, the analyses on which it is based, and the stories it produces tell us a lot about current reality and the ways in which the stronger systems exert their dominium. However, in my opinion, it does not embrace the whole reality.

---

[4] Michel Foucault, *Sorvegliare e punire: la nascita della prigione, traduzione di Alcesti Tarchetti* (Torino: Einaudi, 1976); Michel Foucault, *Microfisica del potere* (Torino: Einaudi, 1977).

[5] Byung-Chul Han, *L'espulsione dell'Altro* (Milano: Nottetempo, 2017), p. 25; Vedi anche, *Psychopolitik: Neoliberalismus und die neuen Machttechniken* (Frankfurt: Fischer, 2014).—trad. Federica Buongiorno, *Psicopolitica* (Milano: Nottetempo, 2016).

The complexity of the world cannot be reduced to a single logic. On the contrary, it can be described with various models, each of which may be more or less effective in helping us to understand some aspects. However, like all models, neither can this one explain everything. Reality contains what it shows us, but a lot more besides.

If we do not consider this limit to be intrinsic to every description, what appears is a reality subject to a single logic: in this case, a society controlled by omniscient, infallible apparatuses. If, on the other hand, we recognize complexity, we see a reality resting on various logics and apparatus that may be very powerful but not omniscient and infallible. We can also see that in the multiplicity of possible realities and in the flaws of the organs of control collocate the local discontinuities I have been talking about, meaning the possibility for human beings to use their resources in terms of creativity and capability to do things in a different way from that expected. Ultimately, the scenario of a control society may help us to recognize the traps that exist in the world we live in and take them into account. But this should not prevent us from seeing that the reality may also be something else, and more importantly, it may also offer opportunities.

This second way of seeing things, which is also my own, collocates in a line of reasoning chiefly expounded by Michel Certeau in the 1980s, and which can be taken up again today and updated to take into account what has happened in the meantime, in terms of social and technological innovation and more generally in terms of vision of the world.

Transgressive tactics and strategies. Over thirty years ago, with his book *The Practice of Everyday Life*, De Certeau[6] highlighted the frequency of acts of resistance to proposed models in people's everyday lives and their creativity in interpreting and adapting to their own use what they are offered. From here he went on to introduce the concept of "productive consumption":

---

[6] Michel de. Certeau, *The Practice of Everyday Life*, trans. Steven Rendall (Berkeley: University of California Press, 1984).

an activity by which a consumer becomes a producer of new meanings. In other words, he becomes an actor capable of inventing everyday life, thanks to tactics that lead him to make original and unexpected use of what the system of goods made available to him. It seems to me that these observations are still completely valid, but they need updating.

Immediately after De Certeau focused on the figure of the active consumer, this concept was fully recognized in marketing, with the consequent attempt to co-opt it into company strategies. The results of this move need discussing, but this is now an ancient story. In the meantime, with the spread of networks and social media, the number of people involved in various ways in producing content has grown exponentially, effectively becoming an integral part of production processes. In short, the active consumer has been replaced by the producer of contents, with all the resulting positive and negative implications.

At the same time, social innovation has brought a new generation of social actors into the open, capable of inventing everyday life with actions the result of which is not a tactical adjustment of the existent, but a system change on a local scale: leaving the car for the bike, leaving large-scale distribution to create direct relations with producers, transforming the life of a condominium by introducing elements of collaborative living, and so on.

All this shows ways of thinking and doing things that call for an update on some observations and concepts introduced by De Certeau thirty years ago. The figure of coproducer that he proposed is that of an essentially isolated subject who may be active and reactive, but who remains caged in a production and consumption system that he can only modify but not radically change. What social innovation now proposes instead is an individual who breaks out of the cage, redefines the problem, uses the existent in a different sense frame, and enables totally new ways of being and doing things. In effect, for De Certeau, the everyday inventions that the coproducers were able to come up with were tactical. They concerned the capability of single actors to move in the given context, seizing the opportunities that came up to introduce local modifications, without really calling into question the system in which they occurred and the power relations on which they were based. Vice versa, system changes, which De Certeau calls strategic because they entail the transformation of power relations between the system actors, were for him the field of intervention for the institutions or whoever held the power to apply them.

It seems to me that social innovation breaks with this scheme; what the actors involved make are not tactical choices but are, to all intents and purposes, strategic choices. Admittedly, this happens on a local scale but, nevertheless, they are capable of generating large-scale system changes. Such major changes are in reality prepared and made possible by the multiplication, interaction, and consolidation over time of small-scale radical changes.

I would now like to add that this happens *both* when particularly active people invent and put into practice an initiative that is (locally) completely new (like the group of farmers who brought the first farmers' markets in Montevarchi to life) *and* when the success of the initiative leads it to stabilize and institutionalize, thus becoming (locally) normal: a kind of normality that remains transformative because it counteracts the orientation of the large-scale dominant system. To make this affirmation clearer, I shall return briefly to the transformative social innovation (Chapter 1), which underlies everyday-life policies, and introduce the concept of innovation trajectory.

From activism to transformative normality. The path that led to the farmers' market in Montevarchi with which I started this chapter is a good example of an innovation trajectory. This case can be generalized: every social innovation starts with a group of people, a creative community,[7] that invents and puts into practice

---

[7] Anna Meroni, *Creative Communities. People Inventing Sustainable Ways of Living* (Polidesign: Milano, 2007); A. Meroni and D. Selloni, "Design for Social Innovators," in S. Walker, T. Cassidy, M. Evans, Holroyd A. Twigger, and J. Jung (eds.), *Design Roots* (London: Bloomsbury Academic, 2018).

new ways of being and doing things. Then, if the idea is a good one, it may evolve from the initial heroic stage into a mature form in which the proposal is made accessible to a wider, less committed public. This evolution may occur in various ways, leading to different results depending on the context in which they take place and the intentions and design capability of their promoters. To discuss this we shall look at another case: the collaborative housing project presented in the previous chapter, with its passage from the heroic cohousing initiatives to mature forms of collaborative housing, and more besides, as we shall see.

The initial cohousing experiences in the second half of the last century resulted from the group actions of people who were highly motivated, not only as far as concerns the practical value of collaborative housing but also for its potential social and environmental implications. It was the force of these two motivations that enabled them to invent new models of living and, in the face of all kinds of difficulty, put them into practice. In doing this, they also activated a far-reaching innovative process: by making the advantages of collaborative housing visible and tangible, they increased the number of people potentially interested. This in turn also drove people to look for ever easier solutions to adopt, ones that were more feasible for people with less time and energy to invest in the activity. At the same time, political decision makers and building companies started to recognize the social value of such ways of living, and their correspondence to people's real needs, and created more suitable financial and regulatory environments to make them possible. In short, the initial ideas gradually evolved toward greater accessibility, producing a kind of *transformative normality*:[8] a form of collaborative living that has become normal for those living it in the context where they

---

[8] One formal definition of *transformative normality* could be the following: ways of thinking and doing things that become normal in a given context (i.e., normal for those who adopt them), but which are far from normal in other contexts. Transformative normality is therefore a local discontinuity, in contrast with dominant practice in the wider socio-technical systems in which they collocate.

are, but which is still a radically different way of living from that proposed in the majority of other housing contexts.

Recent research carried out in various European cities by Fondazione Housing Sociale (an Italian social housing foundation)[9] highlights the way in which the housing sector, and the way people live the city in general, is changing: ways of living based on the flexible sharing of spaces and services, which in the past were created and used only by active minorities, are now adopted by more people who recognize them as being more coherent with the fluid world we are living in. This is bringing about unprecedented residential and working typologies: "Housing types are many and in continual evolution, and they take shapes and modalities that blur the confines between what is a home and what is an office or a service area … today we can hire a desk in an office, rooms for a period, collective kitchens for a dinner, and everything always within a physical and relational environment that extends and completes our experience."[10]

The phenomenon described here demonstrates something more than what we have said so far about innovation trajectories. It tells us that they may lead to mature solutions that not only maintain their social qualities but may interweave together to produce new communities and new urban organisms (such as

---

[9] This research was also the material on which *New Urban Body* (*Esperienze di Generazione Urbana*), an exhibition curated by Giordana Ferri, was created. The exhibition took place in the Triennale di Milano between November 2017 and January 2018.

[10] Introduction to the exhibition *New Urban Body* (*Esperienze di Generazione Urbana*), La Triennale, Milano (http://www.newurbanbody.it/la-mostra). As well as by the integration of diverse functions (living, working, meeting people, and having fun), these new urban organisms are characterized by the diversity of people living in them, by their use throughout the day, by their promotion and management by various actors (public, private, local organizations, and ordinary citizens), by their various offer conditions (free, by consumption, by contract), by their use at various timescales (by the hour, day, month, or year), by their operation at various levels (local and global, physical and virtual), and by their orientation toward financial, social, and environmental sustainability.

those described in the research results we are talking about): multiple entities in which homes, services, production, and cultural activities combine to generate unprecedented spaces, complex hybrid spaces that, because of their complexity, can become centers of urban regeneration and help reconstruct the city's social fabric.

However, things do not always go as described above. The original ideas and practices may also follow other trajectories as they mature; they may evolve losing, or decidedly betraying, the motivations that had generated them and the social value they had produced through their initial idea. Still on the theme of living, we can see that as well as the positive cases we have mentioned, there are others that have evolved in the opposite direction: collocating the proposal for shared services in a totally commercial prospective and, in the name of a misinterpreted security or status, segregating people in protected, fenced off residential complexes. By doing this, they set in motion ways of living that are totally opposed to the original idea of collaborative living.

Transforming

Innovation trajectories and design choices. To sum up, experience tells us that successful initial ideas evolve and transform. The fact that, as far as their social significance is concerned, they may maintain some of the original characteristics are only one of the possibilities and not a trajectory that can be taken for granted. Rather, without constant, careful redesigning and step-by-step re-orientation, it is probable that an innovation trajectory will take the direction that today appears easiest: in the name of productive efficiency, it will annul or negate the initial social value. The result of this will be that instead of offering life projects a field of possibilities that is open to sustainable ways of doing things, it will attract them in directions (and toward everyday-life policies) that appear as new as they are in fact debatable (if not actually negative) on an environmental and social plane. The discussion previously of protected neighborhoods is one example, but unfortunately there are also many others.

To debate this issue, I shall refer to another field of activity, taking as an example another well-known case: that of cars shared by people traveling the same route. This is carpooling, originally intended as a way of saving on transport costs but also of socializing and reducing traffic. This simple, but potentially very effective, idea has evolved in various directions exploiting the possibilities given by digital technology and geolocalization. Digital platforms have emerged that in various ways support encounters and car sharing between people who know each other, or could know each other, and who travel the same route every day (thus making more efficient the spontaneous car sharing that has always existed among people who live in the same neighborhood and work or study in another area of the city). While this is the evolutionary line that offers more continuity with the original idea, the more successful one is the line that ultimately counteracts all the social and environmental values on which the original idea was based. All that remains is the basic idea of putting potential drivers and passengers in contact, doing so simply and cheaply by way of a specially designed digital platform. The world champion in this field is obviously the Californian Uber (today threatened in its monopoly by the Chinese Didi).[11]

Looking at these examples from the point of view of life projects, there is a huge distance between the original idea of carpooling, put into practice by groups of friends or neighbors, and the global platforms like Uber. In the original carpooling idea, everyone in the car feels in an equal position, even

---

[11] Uber and Didi Chuxing are companies that provide a private car transport service by means of an application that directly connects passengers and drivers. Uber has its headquarters in California and has spread all over the world. Didi holds the monopoly in China, where it has bought Uber China, and is now expanding to other countries.

though at a particular moment only one is driving and making his car available to others. To all intents and purposes, it is a collaborative activity in which the life projects of various people meet and intertwine with equal dignity and equal power (the informal rules of good behavior require the first passenger to sit next to the driver, as if to say, "We are all peers"). Quite on the contrary, evolving toward the great platforms, there is a clear difference in roles and status between the driver, the passengers, and the platform manager. The platform manager holds all the power. The user-passengers become normal clients, who are offered a service that, from their point of view, may be very efficient and cheap but totally void of any relational value (in this case the passenger sits on the backseat, marking the difference in roles). Lastly, there is the user-driver who ends up in the role of a temporary worker, with no job security and no rights, totally dependent on the platform owner.

The example of mobility platforms can be generalized. The same model has been adopted in other fields: for example, flat sharing, product delivery, and job supply and demand. In practice, it has extended and is rapidly spreading to all fields in which disintermediation, together with the geolocalization of the actors involved and the possibility of digital payment, can produce a service that is efficient from the user point of view and profitable for the platform owner. In all these cases, we are talking about *a platform economy*.

The platform economy and the new cooperative movement. As it is presented today, the platform economy is highly problematical for various reasons. The first and most evident is that if appropriate regulatory antibodies are not introduced into networks, the principle of winner-takes-all will always prevail. For this reason such platforms are rapidly becoming global monopolies. Let's take a closer look.

The winner-takes-all principle is a perverse property of networks by which whoever does something a little better than the others quickly and easily dominates the global market. It is perverse because, as we are seeing, it generates monsters: worldwide monopolies of dimensions so huge as to appear ahuman. But that is not all. A second great problem with these digital, global, and private platforms has rapidly emerged: people who base their work and economic survival on their use become entirely dependent on them, in the sense that their existence is totally at the mercy of the platform owners. This makes their lives extremely precarious: the new workers in the platform economy are digital laborers rendering micro-services to anyone requesting them, when and as requested, with no continuity or guarantees for the future.

Confronted with this enormous problem brought by the platform economy as we know it now, an original movement of criticism and alternative proposals[12] has emerged. The underlying idea is that the social disaster generated by platforms, and the disintermediation of which they are the instrument, is not caused by the platforms themselves but by the organizations that have taken possession of them. The problem is said to be the monopoly these organizations hold over the fields of activity in which the platforms are applied and the lack of rights for the people who base their work on them. Therefore, what needs to be done is to imagine and create local but interconnected platforms that belong to the people who use them. This has led to the proposal to update the old idea of cooperatives and build new cooperatives based on the possession of the platforms they operate with, and vice versa to create platforms that it is possible for the cooperatives of their users to own.

---

[12] In the debate about the sharing economy, which has had so much space over the last few years, there are those who say we should move from the initial slogan "Sharing is owning" to another stating "Owning Is the New Sharing," with reference to local platforms owned by those who use them. Scholz, Trebor (December 5, 2014). "Platform Cooperativism vs. the Sharing Economy." *Medium*. Retrieved December 10, 2016; Trebor Scholz, *Uberworked and Underpaid: How Workers Are Disrupting the Digital Economy* (New York City: Polity, 2016"; Nathan Schneider (December 21, 2014), "Owning Is the New Sharing." *Shareable*. Retrieved December 10, 2016; Mayo Fuster Morell (September 2012), "Horizontes del procomún digital" (PDF). Retrieved April 25, 2017.

This is certainly an interesting perspective that indicates a direction in which to go to improve the working conditions of those who depend on them and hence introduce principles of democracy and equity into their management. However, to recover the collaborative character of the original idea, and bring the platforms back into the ambits of collaborative projects, I believe it is necessary to take another step. In my opinion, we need to consider not only the issue of worker ownership, fundamental as that aspect certainly is, but also the relational value and the shared social commons produced in the interaction between different actors. In other words, I believe that criticism of the current platform economy should unite the issue of ownership of the platform itself with that of the quality of relationships established or that could be established through its use.

Sharing economy and collaborative economy. The debate about platforms, their workings, and the new economy they create collocates within a wider debate over a phenomenon, engendered by the social and technological innovation of recent years, that has led to the blossoming of a host of innovative economic models, often called *the sharing economy.* With time, however, it became evident that for many of these models, and for the sharing economy in general, their innovative character had no corresponding social value. Indeed it was rather the opposite, and the platform economy (which is one aspect of the sharing economy) is a clear example of this. The issue has been amply discussed.[13] I would just like to observe that if the sharing economy has rapidly lost its social character in many of its applications, this was caused by the way these collaborative

---

[13] "Sharing economy" is a broad term that has covered a series of different meanings in recent years. Arun Sundararajan, *The Sharing Economy* (Cambridge, MA: MIT Press, 2016); Rachel Botsman and Roo Rogers, *What's Mine Is (Y)ours: The Rise of Collaborative Consumption* (New York: Harper Collins, 2010); Tiziano Bonini and Guido Smorto (eds.), *Sharable! L'economia della condivisione* (Roma: Edizioni di Comunità, 2017).

practices evolved or rather regressed within it. Since producing the relational values proper to collaboration costs time and attention (see Chapter 2), the collaborative dimension has gradually been reduced to zero (as we have seen in the case of mobility platforms). This has happened in the name of service efficiency for the client and, above all, in response to the request by investors to maximize the profitability of the platform itself.

In the light of what has happened, I believe it is useful to update the terminology and talk about *sharing economy* only when it refers to something that is pooled, without it implying anything in particular in relational terms. On the other hand, when the relational dimension is present and plays an important role, I think we should talk about *collaborative economy*: an economy in which not only the means are shared (as in the sharing economy) but also the ends. To be more precise, "the collaborative economy is defined as practices and business models based on horizontal networks and participation of a community."[14] It focuses on "shared ownership of individual property, co-management of services, co-production of manufactured goods and, therefore, hinges more on collaboration than on sharing."[15] The second part of this definition is significant for two reasons: for what it says, highlighting important aspects of the collaborative economy,

---

[14] Ouishare (http://ouishare.net/en/about/collaborative_economy).

[15] Vittorio Bugli, Assessore alla Presidenza della Regione Toscana, Preface to *Libro Verde CollaboraToscana. Per un'agenda regionale sull'economia collaborativa e i beni comuni* (Firenze: Regione Toscana, 2017). This book is based on a research with the same title, done by GovLab (scientific management) and SocioLab (general organization and management. As well as giving a clear and up-to-date framework to the question of collaborative economy, il Libro Verde offers advice on the theme and outlines a plan for experimenting with the collaborative economy in Tuscany entitled "Piano di sperimentazione sull'economia collaborativa in Toscana," which identifies twelve main aims corresponding to as many fields of activity including mobility, housing, agriculture, and hospitality.

and also for whom it says it. The sentence quoted is actually an extract from the preface to the Libro Verde CollaboraToscana, a document produced by the Tuscan regional government and the result of field research in Tuscany. As stated in the subtitle, it is intended to be "a regional agenda for the collaborative economy and the commons." This document and the work preceding it are important because they show how the idea and practices of the collaborative economy are spreading and becoming objects of attention even at institutional level.

On my part, I believe that this attention and the institutional experimentation that should follow are what the collaborative economy needs today. It is a question of experimenting with forms of governance that connect bottom-up collaborative practices—as expressions of active citizenship—with those of the other social actors involved or who could be involved (e.g., third sector, companies, universities, and public bodies). In this perspective, the role of the public sector is delicate but fundamental: in order for collaborative economy practices to express their innovative potential to the full, without veering in socially unsustainable directions, they need to be accompanied by appropriate forms of governance. However, since such forms do not yet exist, they must become the object of institutional experimentation.[16]

Collaboration, efficiency, and relational value. The collaborative economy can be discussed and supported from various points of view. The one that is most consonant with the theme of this book is one that focuses on collaboration itself, particularly on the collaborative encounters between the people involved and then on the single individual in response to the question: "Why choose to collaborate when I could choose not to?" The classic economist used to answer this kind of question from the point of view of a subject who makes "rational" choices. For the economist in question, this meant

---

[16] I believe this is also the sense of the final part of Assessore Bugli's preface to the Libro Verde mentioned above. Vittorio Bugli, ibid.

"according to his personal economic advantage." It followed that this "economic man" would never have occupied his time in doing something that did not have a return in terms of personal advantage. However, this totally economic man does not exist. History in general and the recent history of social innovation in particular show us that people make their decisions in other ways (also) using other forms of rationality and (also) expressing other interests. Thus today, the answer from the innovative economist comes from the standpoint of a person who considers himself, the community, and the society as a whole[17] when he chooses.

However, in my opinion, this change in the reference figure is important, but not enough to answer my initial question about why our protagonist should choose to collaborate. It tells us that people may (also) choose to collaborate but not why, when, and in what conditions they do so (and in which they don't). To give a real answer, we need to put ourselves in the shoes of the person who has to make the choice, looking carefully at his motivations, the difficulties he faces, and what results he really recognizes as such. Doing this, we are led to acknowledge that the relational values that a collaborative encounter produces have a cost in terms of the time and energy required and the perceived constraints on individual freedom (since establishing a relationship always entails a certain commitment). I have already mentioned this in Chapter 2, but here I would like to add that, in making his own choices, our protagonist must

---

[17] For Christian Iaione, professor of public law and expert in the commons, the shift from the market economy to the collaborative economy corresponds to a change in the protagonist from *homo oeconomicus* to one which, with reference to the thinking of Hanna Arendt, he describes as *mulier activa*: a person who gives sense to his or her own life by acting in public space and collaborating with others in the common interest. Gregorio Arena, Christian Iaione, *L'età della condivisione. La collaborazione tra cittadini e amministrazione per i beni comuni* (Carrocci Editore: Roma, 2015), pp. 14, 15. Hannah Arendt, *The Human Condition*, 2nd edn. (Chicago: University of Chicago Press, 1958).

consider two alternatives: whether to seek maximum efficiency and accessibility (seen from his own standpoint, meaning that of the person who will benefit from the results of the proposed solution) or accept a reduction in benefit and commit part of his resources to producing relational values and social commons. Obviously, there is no formula that enables us to indicate once and for all how this choice will be made, that is, within a given field of possibility, the way in which each person seeks an appropriate balance between efficiency and relational values, which must be determined case by case.

We shall now change our observation point and consider the characteristics of the ecosystem within which this choice is made. The best situation is one that offers our protagonist various possibilities (in terms of combinations of the efficiency and relational values produced), allowing him to choose what is more congenial to him thus giving him the possibility of choosing from solutions that give access to different combinations of accessibility and relational values and therefore different equilibriums. The cases of mature social innovation introduced so far—the farmers' market, the assisted cohousing, and the cooperative and relational platforms—are just some examples of this offer of feasible compromises; other possibilities, characterized by other equilibriums, could be found.

Having said this, what certainly should not occur is the nullification of one of the poles. If we try to maintain the production of relational values, without improving the accessibility and efficiency of a proposal, it will tend to close in on itself, meaning on the small group of highly committed people who started it. That way it will inevitably die out when their energy fails (it is impossible to be social heroes forever!). Vice versa, seeking only efficiency and accessibility leads to the loss of the collaborative nature of what is proposed, turning it into an initiative that may even be considered innovative and successful but which has no social value.

So, a social innovation trajectory that still maintains its transformative characteristics when it has reached the normalization stage implies that it transforms this polarity into a positive, generative tension capable of producing an infinite number of solutions, each characterized by a different balance between the two poles and therefore by different forms of collaboration.

To conclude, I would like to return to my accolade to lightness that concluded the first chapter. Then, I talked about the value of the lightness of contemporary communities and the open, flexible interactions that characterize them—of the fact that they could be built from a "profound perception of what is 'minute, mobile and light,'" as Italo Calvino wrote when talking about lightness in his *American Lessons*.[18] Here, I could say the same thing for the collaboration we are talking about and the policies for everyday life that it leads to.

I will explain myself better: although there is and will always be the need for initiatives based on strong, enthusiastic, militant (in a word: heroic) collaboration, large-scale social transformation will only occur if there are opportunities for accessible, variegated, and light collaboration, in which everyone is able to find their own niche. In short, we need to extend and multiply the islands of transformative normality we have been talking about and make them accessible to a growing number of people, so that they have the possibility of choosing to live in the way they prefer. In doing so, they will be able to bring their own contribution, in terms of everyday-life policies, to the transition toward sustainability.

Everyday-life policies, other policies, and other democracies. At the end of Chapter 2, I wrote that these everyday-life policies are the preconditions for drawing the world out of the catastrophic trajectory it is set on, but they are certainly not enough on their own. Now, we have seen that they require the contribution of experts and public institutions in order to create a favorable environment for them to emerge and evolve in the best possible way.

---

[18] Italo Calvino, *Six Memos for the Next Millennium* (Cambridge: Harvard University Press, 1988), pp. 8 and 9 (English version).

Social activists are needed to widen the field of possibilities, and experts, institutions, and enterprises, with common objectives, are needed to make them easily accessible, creating and consolidating new areas of transformative normality. We need to create a mesh of design actions and activities operating in different ways on different scales. All this together can be seen as a new form of democracy, or more precisely, as a new ramification of participatory democracy: a project-centered democracy in which the everyday-life policies we have been talking about have a role that gives a voice to the life projects of people and communities and at the same time embraces and consolidates their transformative capabilities.

4

Project-Centered Democracy: Ecosystems of Ideas and Projects

There is always someone in the bar in the central square of Ambra, the nearest village to where I live, and there are always discussions. We talk about ourselves, about other people, about the world. About football, obviously, and about politics, though less than we used to. The square is also the place where a variety of social networks intercept and everything that goes on in the village goes through here.

The square in Ambra, in itself, has nothing in particular that distinguishes it from what many other squares in Italy have traditionally been. What makes it special in its own way is that places like this are becoming increasingly rare. Obviously, Ambra is not out of the world and so, as the old people say, it is not what it used to be: the prevailing tendency toward individualism is at work here too. However, here a bridge between the communities of the past and those that may be the communities of the future looks possible. If we look more carefully at what happens in the bar and square in Ambra, we can see that the people meeting there also take part in various communities associated with their work, interests, age, and origins (the original residents, those by choice, immigrants from various ethnic groups, and tourists). Each of these groups has its own life and autonomy, but here in Ambra they also manage to meet each other and produce the community of people who feel "part of the place." This is a community that has a tie with that of the past but is no longer what it used to be: it is an open, flexible, contemporary community that has a tie with the place. It is a community of place with permeable, modifiable borders.

I have already written about these forms of community, of how they exist not as a natural given but as a collateral effect of interweaving projects. Here, I would like to add that for the same reasons, this square is also a fundamental component of a way of understanding democracy and putting it into practice. But what democracy are we talking about?

In Ambra, we obviously vote (though with waning enthusiasm). However, it is also clear here that democracy is not only about going to vote. Democracy is also the possibility for discussion and collective action. Considering it is such a small village, Ambra offers ample opportunity for this: there is the Filarmonica, which runs the cinema-theater, the band, music, and singing lessons for the schools; the Proloco (in Italy, a local volunteer association seeking to promote and develop a place) organizes numerous entertainment activities; the Misericordia (in Italy, a volunteer confraternity offering ambulance services and assistance to the sick and elderly) and the Sports Association. Ambra also shares many other associations with villages in the vicinity, and these concern young people, art, tourism, agriculture, and the environment. There is also the parish church and what is left of the political parties.

Saying that there are many possibilities for discussion and collective actions in Ambra does not of course mean that everyone takes part in them. Every association has its group of activists who are joined by others in different ways, playing various roles. However, even altogether they do not represent everyone. Thus, they cannot be seen as an expression of representative democracy. Nevertheless, as well as producing tangible results on various issues, this wealth of associations does help democracy. By triggering conversations, it produces the commons that constitute the precondition for democracy: language and discourse; the ability to listen and compare ideas. And they feed the formal, representative dimension of democratic discussion with projects and ideas, keeping it in constant dialogue with what is proposed by this mesh of activities, which I shall call project-centered democracy. Even though there are no longer the great unifying narratives of the past, there is still a shared vision of democracy, in the sense given when all such initiatives as those previously listed are taken together, as a whole. So, although it is true that we meet less often to discuss politics in the square, in traditional fashion (to discuss things that someone else—in the town hall, in the regional government, or at national level—has done or should do for us), we do still discuss extensively about what we intend to do: about ideas that, in principle, could be realized by ourselves. The result is a complex democracy in which formal democracy encounters participatory and project-centered democracy, influencing each other and creating a virtuous circle.

Commoning

The complex nature of democracy. "Democracy" is a word of many meanings: its etymology takes us back to the theme of the government of people (from the ancient Greek *démos*, "people," and *krátos*, "power") whereby, in its original meaning, democracy is understood as a system of government in which power is exercised directly or indirectly by "the people," meaning by citizens. A practical translation of this first definition leads us to two further terms required to describe how the people exercise their government. One is "liberty" and the other "equality," where liberty means the possibility for everybody to express their own opinions and to seek happiness as they prefer. This brings with it the question of human rights, which is nowadays inextricably tied to democracy. On the other hand, we have the quest for equality, which brings with it the question of the fair distribution of economic and cultural resources. However, equality also means admitting that individual freedom has its limits. It has to accept the limits given by the freedom of others, which also includes the fair distribution of resources and services necessary to enjoy it.

Liberty and equality refer to two differing political traditions: the liberal tradition, which affirms the importance of rules, the separation of powers, and individual freedom; and the socialist tradition, which stresses the fair distribution of resources and power, that is, equality.

The quest for liberty and equality is counteractive: obtaining an increase in one inevitably produces a reduction in the other and vice versa. However, the tension between these two poles is not necessarily a problem for democracy. As the political analyst Chantal Mouffe wrote, this tension "creates a space in which this confrontation is kept open, power relations are always being put into question and no victory can be final."[1]

For the American philosopher John Dewey, democracy is the social environment that best enables the development of individual energies. This is because, being in a state of perennial instability, as we have seen, it calls for a continual ability to adapt to and reread reality.[2] Democracy can therefore be described as a space where it is possible to dialogue and make decisions, accepting a set of rules, thanks to which everybody has, or should have, the same possibility of expressing and influencing results. The way of arriving at these rules may be very different. To do so requires having available a set of capabilities and values, which for Dewey are education,

[1] Chantal Mouffe, *The Democratic Paradox* (London: Verso, 2000), p. 15.
[2] John Dewey, "Emerson—The Philosopher of Democracy," *International Journal of Ethics* 13 (July 1903), 405–413.

interest for the public good, critical ability, and the willingness to collaborate and share with others. On the other hand, the diffusion of these capabilities and values in society is, to all intents and purposes, part of its commons. A part of its commons that is so important for democracy that, in the end, we can say that democracy itself, like all the capabilities and values that make it possible, is a common good.[3]

This observation brings with it others that are just as important. If democracy is like this, then as for all commons, the rule applies that it cannot be designed and produced like other products. It cannot be imposed or taken away. It can only emerge from the workings of an entire community over time (Chapter 1). From here derives another important observation: democracy, like all commons, cannot be fully achieved. It can only be approached through a process that democratizes the society on which it occurs. Just as *commons* are built through *commoning*, meaning the activity of building commons, to promote democracy we need to shift our attention from the noun to the verb: from the word "democracy," which refers to an abstract idea of how things should be, to the concrete processes of "democratizing." Thanks to these processes, any society may move toward democracy (or as, at this moment, seems to be the case in many parts the world, it may regress from the levels of democracy previously reached, activating

---

[3] The background to this chapter owes much to Carlo Donolo, and particularly to his book, *Il sogno del buon governo, Apologia del regime democratico* (Milano: Anabasi, 1992). When I read it twenty-five years ago, it opened a window onto the relationship between democracy and complexity. On reading it again now, it seems to me that everything Donolo says in that book is still extraordinarily applicable to current circumstances. In view of the growing crisis in democracy, I have recently returned to this topic, also thanks to conversations with Victor Margolin after his lecture at the Carnegie Mellon University in 2012. Victor Margolin, "Design and Democracy in a Troubled World," Lecture at School of Design, Carnegie Mellon University, April 11, 2012 (http://www.democracy-design.org/wp-content/uploads/2017/05/Design-and-Democracy-in-a-Troubled-World-.pdf).

processes of de-democratization). So, in principle, any society may democratize and do so following its own particular path, moving from its own particular point of departure and the opportunities deriving from it (and fostering some issues more than others).

A regime capable of learning. By its very nature, democracy is the terrain of consensus-building and commoning, both time-consuming processes. It is also the place of conflicts and mediation, and thus of time-wasting, if time is considered only in terms of technocratic efficiency.

Nowadays, it seems to many that this intrinsic viscosity of democracy is in stark contrast to the urgency of the issues we must and will have to deal with and therefore with that of the seemingly urgent need to make strong, rapid decisions. This is giving rise to growing support for authoritarian forms that in the name of efficiency are prepared to sacrifice the fundamental principles of liberty, equality, and the balance of powers.

These proposals, and the way of seeing things they derive from, must be counteracted, not only for ethical reasons and on principle but also because they have been shown not to work. Both theory and past experience tell us that democracy is the only regime able to sustain humanity in the difficult, transitional stage in which we find ourselves, with all the risks and difficulties that this entails—for example, the way in which awareness of environmental limits, criticism of nuclear energy production, and recognition of organic agriculture and local food have all emerged over the past decades as minority positions. The existence of such minorities was possible, despite many difficulties, within the ambits of democratic regimes whose prevailing ideas, at the time, were oriented in very different directions. None of this was possible in authoritarian regimes that, in the name of efficiency in achieving objectives that seemed to be priorities at the time, prevented the formulation and growth of other ideas, including those that might later prove useful, and even necessary, in tackling unexpected events and unforeseeable changes in the context.

On the contrary, we can observe that because it accepts and cultivates diversity, democracy is able to bring out alternatives in moments of need. In other words, democracy is a resilient regime (Chapter 1).

At the same time, because it is by nature open and tolerant, democracy can liberate the creativity, skills, and, at the end of the day, the project-making ability with which human beings are endowed. Furthermore, it can enhance another of their capabilities: the ability to weigh their experiences and, when confronted with evidence and/or convincing arguments, to change their idea or produce a new one and thus create knowledge. Because of this, democracy is not merely a neutral tool for social conversation; it is also a *regime capable of learning*. In other words, it is capable of transforming individual and small-group experiences into values and behavior shared by the entire community: commons, therefore, that constitute the ground on which new activities, collaborative projects, and democratic practices can flourish.

For this reason, although it is undeniable that there is an urgent need to change the state of things and the direction of its development, the way to do so is not the brusque way of authoritarian regimes, neither is it the exasperated search for rapidity typical of technocratic efficientism. Instead, we must give democracy its time, accelerating as much as possible but giving it the possibility to produce or reproduce the commons on which it is based and on which is based the possibility for all of us to learn to live, and possibly live better, on this small, densely populated planet.

The dimensions of the crisis. Today, democracy is in crisis, a crisis that is made evident by the success of democratic–authoritarian regimes in many parts of the world and, even more surprisingly, by the ethical and cultural involution underway in Europe and the United States (of which what is happening around the migration question is the most evident aspect). However, dramatic as they are, these phenomena appear to be the effect rather than the cause of the crisis, which has deep roots reaching further back in history.

The rules, values, and institutions of the democracy we know today, and of which we see the crisis, were produced in the past. They were born on the centuries-long road to modernization traveled by Western societies and emerged in particular from the political context and values of the second half of the twentieth century. Since then much has changed: globalization as we have known it until now has led to the marginalization of a growing number of people, lacerating the social pacts that constituted the very basis of democracy. Furthermore, by imposing the idea that there was no alternative to its neoliberal models, this globalization has dictated that its directives be followed with no margin of freedom, almost as though they were natural laws. Thus, it has annulled the first and fundamental pillar in the definition of democracy: the one that indicates democracy as the power of people. Nowadays, we see every day that people, at all levels of representation, have less and less power to decide what to do and how to do it. This, it is said, is because there are no economically feasible alternatives and the only conceivable future is to continue the current state of things.

It has happened in fact that in the evolution toward ultra-centralized systems, decisions are made in an increasingly opaque way and by institutions and economic actors that lack any democratic investiture to do so. As a consequence, people have the impression that democratic discussion is useless because, at the end of the day, decisions are made by others in other places. It seems to me that this is the main ground on which the crisis of democracy has developed: if there are no alternatives to choose from, there is no point in discussing and deliberating. If, in the name of automatisms in the economic systems (which are really only the shameless imposition of the interests of a privileged elite on the majority), the field of action is reduced to little or nothing, there can be no democracy. Consequently, I believe that the regeneration of democracy must start from here: from the radical affirmation that democracy must give more "power to the people." In order to do this, it must put liberty and equality, human rights and social equity, together in a creative manner. This means tackling the crisis of democracy by promoting a great season of experimentation: democratic experimentation that makes best use of the opportunities that social innovation and technology can offer.

Experimenting

Toward a distributed democracy. If people must have power, there must be questions on which they can really make decisions and arenas in which they can do so. In practice, this means that decision-making power on various questions must be given to the communities involved. However, to do this, the questions to be discussed and decided must themselves have a local dimension on which choices can have a direct impact.

In other words, it is not only a case of discussing questions on a local level that will then be decided and put into action by central organisms. Instead, production and service systems need to be developed whose local functioning depends mainly on local subsystems, endowed with autonomy and determined by choices made and carried out locally. This means shifting from the centralized hierarchical systems prevailing today to *distributed systems*: socio-technical systems consisting of a network of interconnected but relatively autonomous elements over which the local communities have the real possibility of deciding.

Robin Murray describes this transition (which for him is a paradigm change) as follows:

The shift to a network paradigm has the potential to transform the relationship between organisational centres and peripheries. Its distributed systems handle complexity not by standardisation and simplification imposed from the centre, but by distributing complexity to the margins— to households and service users, and in the workplace to local managers and workers. Those at the margins have what those at the centre can never have—a knowledge of detail—the specificity of time, of place, of particular events, and in the consumer's and citizen's case, of need and desire. This is the potential. But to realise it requires new terms of engagement with users, new relations at work, new terms of employment and compensation.[4]

For my part, on other occasions,[5] I have talked amply about this new paradigm and the scenario deriving from it (which I have called the SLOC scenario, where SLOC stands for Small, Local, Open, Connected): a scenario in which the socio-technical systems are capable of tackling complexity because, as Murray writes, they redistribute it to the network nodes. By doing this, it is possible for them to make best use of locally available resources and to learn by experience. Precisely because of this, distributed systems are resilient and sustainable (as opposed to centralized, hierarchical systems that, by their very nature, are intrinsically fragile and unsustainable). To these favorable considerations, I can now add that distributed systems are also a favorable context for democracy: by distributing activities and power to the network nodes, they make arenas possible and accessible for discussion about questions of public interest, and they do so proposing questions on a scale such that they can be debated by the communities immediately interested.

Imagining a transition from systems that are (prevalently) centralized to ones that are (prevalently) distributed is not a utopia. If we observe reality carefully with all its contradictions, we can see that dominant as the centralized system model still is, there are also countertendencies: connectivity and

---

[4] Robin Murray, "Dangers and Opportunity: Crisis and the New Social Economy," NESTA-Provocations, September 2009 (http://www.nesta.org.uk/publications/reports/).

[5] Ezio Manzini, Design, *When Everybody Designs* (Cambridge, MA: MIT Press, 2015). See also Ezio Manzini, "Small, Local, Open and Connected: Design Research Topics in the Age of Networks and Sustainability," *Journal of Design Strategies* 4, no. 1 (Spring 2010).

the miniaturization of numerous devices make the adoption of distributed organizational forms and systems increasingly cheap and convenient. Renewable energies, which are strongly inclined toward distributed systems by their very nature, are the most evident example. Food networks, with the diffusion of their locally based production and consumption systems, are another one. Lastly, with the makers movement and new digital craftspeople we are also witnessing experimentation of the potentialities of distributed systems on the part of manufacturing.[6] To this discussion we can add another, about the prospects of an economy that is distributed too. In doing so, we can introduce issues such as economic democracy, new cooperativism, and regeneration of the commons.

Undoubtedly, at the moment, this paradigm change is only an opportunity and not all the technical and sociocultural innovations I have mentioned will develop in the right direction. Some of them may lose their social value and be channeled into the course of neoliberal ideas and practices. In addition, the local distribution of power and economic resources that distributed systems make possible can bring them well-being and environmental regeneration provided that the area itself is healthy, meaning if it is not under control, as unfortunately so often happens, by power groups or even by actual local mafias. To avoid this danger, which undoubtedly exists, it is necessary that the choices made and the activities that follow be transparent, participatory, and, ultimately, democratic.

We should also say that the same policy of transparency and democratic governance could, in principle, also be applied to centralized systems in order to avoid them being taken over

---

[6] S. Maffei, "Microproduction Everywhere: Defining the Boundaries of the Emerging New Distributed Microproduction Socio-Technical Paradigm, in Social Frontiers," in *The Next Edge of Social Innovation* (London: Nesta, 2013), https://www.scribd.com/document/192022372/Microproduction-everywhere-Social-local-open-and-connected-manufacturing.

by global power groups and mafias as is in fact happening. However, there is a considerable difference between the two models: whereas transparency and democratic management are intrinsically difficult for centralized systems, for distributed systems they are a concrete possibility.

In conclusion, in returning a certain quota of power to local communities, the scenario of distributed systems is the only one that allows the crisis of democracy to be tackled at its deepest roots. Whether and how this will actually be put into practice will depend on a combination of factors. Among these, there is also the one that constitutes the central theme of this book: how people will act and what everyday-life policies they will be capable of putting into practice in the evolving contexts in which we find ourselves operating.

The difficulties of digital democracy. The diffusion of digital technologies and the new media has transformed the entire communicative environment in which democratic processes take place, opening new possibilities on this terrain too, but also challenging the practices that shaped the democracy of the last century. Over ten years ago, Bruno Latour called this possibility the new "democratic atmosphere,"[7] describing it as a hybrid physical and virtual space made of places, networks, platforms, and digital media, which together create a wide variety of public arenas in which to discuss questions of common interest, make decisions, and make them operative. But, as we know, this is not how things have gone. Ten years later, SITRA, an important Finnish research center, writes: "In an age where technology allows us in theory to connect with one another much more deeply, we are in fact witnessing a huge trend in segregation, filter bubbles and homogenisation."[8]

---

[7] Bruno Latour and Peter Weibel, *Making Things Public: Atmospheres of Democracy* (Cambridge, MA: MIT, 2005), pp. 14–43.
[8] Elina Kiiski Kataja, *From the Trials of Democracy towards the Future Participation,* SITRA Memorandum, March 21, 2017.

Indeed, the diffusion of digital technology and the new media is having a devastating effect on traditional forms of democracy and, above all, on the representative democracy that until now has been the fundamental pillar of complex societies. The question is well known and amply debated: digital technology and connectivity allow the construction of delocalized, de-synchronized, and disintermediated social forms. To put it more simply, people can now interact without mediators, independently of the places they are in and the moment in which they choose to do so, hence the crisis of traditional political organizations and representative democracy. Moreover, this connectivity has also led to a short circuit between these unprecedented possibilities for disintermediation and the traditional idea of direct democracy. The outcome is the emergence of a scenario of permanent direct democracy: one in which everybody, or so they say, has the possibility of expressing themselves about everything in more or less real time.

With or without digital support, direct democracy is certainly of very great value with regard to certain well-specified questions. However, not all matters under discussion are suitable for this kind of treatment, which necessarily simplifies the issue by couching it as a question that can only be answered with a "yes" or a "no." Experience shows us that very few issues can be handled in this way without brutally oversimplifying the situation. It is hardly surprising that—in a moment of crisis in politics and of exasperation with the traditional praxes of democracy—proposals that resort to this direct way of exercising democracy are advanced and meet with success. However, it still remains that basing proposals on an idea of permanent referendum is a mistake. It is a mistake because contrary to what should be done in a moment as difficult as this, they tend to oversimplify the matter in question and trivialize democracy itself.

Where are opinions formed? In the past, opinions were formed in interaction with large organizations (churches, political parties, trade unions, cultural organizations, and so on) that had the task of producing, gathering, and verifying ideas, connecting interlocutors that were otherwise too far apart in time and space. With all their many limits, these organizations played a precise role: they offered grand narratives to refer to and functioned as depositories of experience, knowledge, and expertise that were often incarnated in politicians and experts who were trusted figures. Ultimately, these organizations supplied the arena in which people could compare ideas and form their own opinions on the basis of these conversations.

The proposed digital democracy, on the other hand, calls on everyone to say what they think, but it does not offer occasions in which to cultivate these thoughts, examine them in greater depth, and test them out against other opinions. In short, it does not offer the possibility of confronting complexity with due time for the production of a well-pondered, autonomous opinion. Thus, we fall prey to the ideas of whoever shouts louder, whoever is more capable of compressing proposals into the limited space of a tweet—to the dramatic reduction in the complexity of thought and the limited articulation and depth of opinions that this entails. This is accompanied by a gradual disappearance of public arenas for discussion, poorly substituted by talk shows (where people shout, but fail to discuss) and closed digital communities (where conversations develop between people who think in the same way). The outcome of this is a democracy where people exchange superficial, simplified opinions, more and more often based on the amplification of unfounded ideas and therefore potentially capable of generating monsters.

Yet this worrying scenario is not the whole story. Repeating what has been said in this book about other issues, on looking more closely at the contemporary situation, it emerges that there is also something else, something that we could refer to as lines of experimentation on the theme of digital democracy. Research into these, conducted by the English think tank NESTA, which calls itself "Global Innovation Foundation," concludes by saying that today there are hundreds of tools and platforms in use to facilitate people's commitment in democratic processes. But it also says that there is still a long way to go and that "there are a number of challenges, common to all or most of our case studies, and a number of gaps in the field, which need to be addressed or resolved before digital democracy can reinvigorate and restore the public's trust in our democratic institutions and processes."[9] For my part I would add that for this to happen, it is necessary to bring considerable design capability into play: a creative and political effort that should lead to convergence between the potential of digital technology and the new media, and the practices of social innovation.

With this brief digression on the experimentation underway in the field of digital democracy, my intention was to offer a glimpse of the dynamics in play on this field. However, discussion on this question goes beyond the intentions of this book. Therefore, coherently with what has gone before, I shall try to discuss some aspects adopting the same point of view as in the previous chapters: that of the protagonist of our story, as I introduced him in Chapter 1, immersed in his everyday life and confronted with a democracy that, from his point of view and operating from his point of action, he can exercise directly: participatory democracy. So, from now on, I will focus on this kind of democracy, on its motivations, on the crisis it is going through, and on the opportunities that are opening.

In the conclusion to the NESTA report that I quoted above, when listing the challenges to face, it puts in first place the need to develop "a more nuanced understanding of participation." This is what I would like to contribute to doing now, not only because participatory democracy is important in itself but also because it may be able to regenerate democracy in general.

---

[9] Julie Simon, Theo Bass, Victoria Boelman, and Geoff Mulgan, *Digital Democracy. The Tools Transforming Political Engagement* (London: Nesta, 2017), p. 87.

Participating

Participatory democracy and social innovation. In recent years, the crisis of democracy has not even spared participatory democracy, but I think it has affected it in ways that are different and less disruptive than those we are witnessing in representative democracy. Above all, it has left space for significant signs of vitality and renewal.

To discuss this, we must go back a step. The idea of participatory democracy, and the practices that set it in motion, emerged and consolidated in the last century. For Umberto Allegretti, professor of public law who has done much to promote this theme in Italy, it takes the form of "an interaction … between society and institutions, which aims to produce, case by case, a unitary result attributable to both parties."[10]

This entails the organization of arenas for discussion and exchange between various actors interested in the issue in question. Traditionally, the results of this discussion are the decisions that are then transmitted to other actors who have the power to implement them. The crisis that has struck this kind of democracy can be summarized as follows: the discussion and decision-making activities, which are lengthy, tiring, and weighed down by bureaucratic procedures, often fail to produce actions coherent with what is decided. This obviously makes participation look like a frustrating waste of time and energy.

I believe that today we can start to envisage a way of overcoming these difficulties, and once again it is social innovation that is showing us how. We can see that by converging with technological innovation, social innovation can free resources and create new social forms, thus making it possible to imagine feasible new forms of participation.

---

[10] Umberto Allegretti, ed., *Democrazia partecipativa, Esperienze e prospettive in Italia e in Europa* (Firenze: University Press, 2010), p. 7.

With this in mind, the first thing to do in order to understand these possibilities is to change the idea we normally have of participatory democracy. This means shifting from the idea of participatory democracy as an administrative process to seeing it as a multiplicity of forms of participation: *a participatory ecosystem*[11] whose nature and workings may change from case to case. To discuss this further, I shall go back to the point of view of our protagonist and ask the same simple, naïve question as I did in Chapter 3: Why should he participate? In other words, why should he invest time and energy in participatory actions? Why should he commit himself, imposing constraints on his own freedom of action? The traditional reply is that he should do so out of a sense of civic responsibility: because it is right to take part in decision-making, and in the actions this entails, when it concerns the entire community. I think this reply is still valid, but we should add to it another, one that refers to the motivations and the capabilities of active citizens, as they emerge from a perusal of recent social innovation.

We shall therefore return to the cases mentioned previously. For example, anyone deciding to live collaboratively does so because he thinks sharing residential services is useful, feasible, and economically advantageous. Furthermore, he undoubtedly also recognizes value in sharing with his neighbors and in relational quality in general. Lastly, he very probably thinks that what he is doing is also positive for the neighborhood and the whole city (in that it produces social commons and feeds conversation on this theme with innovative ideas about living better). The same can be said for the farmers and local citizens who create farmers' markets and for all those committed to

---

[11] Giovanni Allegretti, report of the event Democrazia e design, La Triennale di Milano, June 20, 2017. See also P. Spada and G. Allegretti, "Integrating Multiple Channels of Engagement in Democratic Innovations: Opportunities and Challenges," in *Citizen Engagement and Public Participation in the Era of New Media*, volume edited by Marco Adria and Yuping Mao (Heshey, PA, Usa: IGI Global, 2016).

mutual help (in the general frame of collaborative welfare) or who organize neighborhood cultural activities (such as local initiatives of urban regeneration) or again for makers and the new craftspeople (when they are involved in open production activities, distributed over the local area).

A new kind of civic sense. All this highlights an initial lesson that social innovation teaches us: there is a new kind of civic sense, the civic sense of a person who not only takes part in discussion about issues of public interest but also puts into practice and manages what he has discussed. He does so for himself, for the people he collaborates with, and for society as a whole.

The cases offered as examples also teach us another lesson: they are forms of participation in which decision-making is directly linked with putting things into practice. It is not only a question of talking about what to do but also of doing what has been talked about. In other words, the people discussing must also be in a position to actually do what has been discussed. So, the second lesson to be learned from social innovation is this: the composition of the group collaborating to achieve a result defines the field of possibility within which that result can be imagined and achieved (Chapter 2). Or to put it the other way round, having established what we wish to achieve, we must create a group that is able to achieve it. It must not only be willing but also be technically capable and possess the political power to do what has been decided.

This way of proceeding, which to all intents and purposes is a design activity, has the advantage of obtaining tangible results but, in a given context, it also limits the field in which this form of participation can operate. However, this limit is not a fixed one. It depends on the coalition that can be formed. Coalitions composed almost entirely of active citizens, like those that animated most of the cases described thus far, mainly lead to local-scale initiatives. On the other hand, coalitions may also include other actors and therefore other competencies and powers. When this happens, they may aspire to developing much wider projects and thus extend the field in which this participatory model can take place.

More than anywhere else, social innovation is demonstrating the possibility of acting on a large scale in cities. There are numerous examples in which unprecedented coalitions (which include local administrations and active citizens, and also associations, social and commercial enterprises, universities, and research centers) work alongside bottom-up initiatives, giving rise to city-scale projects. In this way, there are cities that have redesigned their mobility systems starting with pedestrians and cyclists; others that are rethinking their food safety, starting with urban and suburban agriculture; yet others are introducing the concept of urban reindustrialization, making space for networks of small industries, traditional artisans, and new digital craftspeople. There are town councils that have made the integration of various projects like those described a fundamental part of their programs, turning them into a single, flexible plan of urban regeneration.[12] These *collaborative cities* (characterized by collaboration between citizens, and between citizens, their associations, and all the other actors present in the local area) may be seen as an *extended enabling system* capable of promoting and supporting initiatives of various kinds and on different scales. They therefore offer their citizens a multiplicity of questions and arenas for discussion and action. This means that the enabling system in collaborative cities also becomes a participatory system. We can take the case of Milan as an example.

Participatory enabling ecosystems. Some years ago, the Milan City Council started a process of "listening to the city" (meaning listening to all the social actors that populate the

---

[12] The European research program URBACT Good Practices presents ninety-seven cases of cities working in this way. See Peter Ramsden, *Experimenting with Governance*, December 12, 2017 (http://urbact.eu/experimenting-governance, http://urbact.eu/experimenting-governance); Francois Jegou and Marcelline Bonneau, *Social Innovation in Cities*, Urbact II, April 2015, Published by Urbact, Saint Denis (France), 2015 (http://urbact.eu/sites/default/files/03_socialinn-web.pdf).

city, including citizens and their organizations) and carefully mapped all the social innovation initiatives underway there.[13] Various strategic goals emerged from here, oriented toward an urban regeneration based on the enhancement of social and cultural resources present in the city. To do this, the city council invested in tangible and intangible infrastructure, support for actor networks, training activities and the development of skills and abilities, and finally in the redevelopment of urban spaces suitable for accommodating these activities. In addition, it worked to create "an atmosphere of trust and collaboration capable of fostering the exchange of information and complex knowledge, the definition of shared rules of behaviour, the development of joint initiatives, and greater involvement of various stakeholders."[14] In short, it worked to produce the necessary social commons to make all the rest possible.

The outcome was the creation of a favorable environment for a large number of social, cultural, sports, and small-business projects to flourish, including community welfare, collaborative living and working, digital craftsmanship, and the creation of business incubators to promote models of collaborative economy. This has contributed greatly to redefining the entire city, making it far more dynamic. What has emerged is a *città dei cittadini* ("city of the citizens") meaning not only a city made *for* its citizens (seen as city users) but also a city made *by* its citizens, in the true sense of the word: a city built by its inhabitants (maybe not in its physical dimension but certainly

---

[13] The process that led to the definition of these strategic objectives started in April 2013, with the organization of a public initiative called "Public Hearing: Verso Milano Smart City." This initiative marked a discontinuity with what had gone before because right after the start, it sought to involve all the actors and to leave them space to be active protagonists. *Libro Bianco di Milano sull'innovazione sociale, Milano*, Aprile 2017 (http://www.milanosmartcity. org/joomla/images/libro%20bianco_innovazione%20sociale.pdf).

[14] Translated from the *Libro Bianco di Milano sull'innovazione sociale, Milano*, Aprile 2017, p. 21 (http://www.milanosmartcity.org/joomla/images/ libro%20bianco_innovazione%20sociale.pdf).

in the relational dimension of its services and organizations). Indeed, while it is true that the results I have described now could never have been achieved without the wide coalitions we have been talking about, it is also true that none of this could have occurred without the active, collaborative participation of those directly concerned.

So, it is in this that the specific characteristics of urban regeneration policies like this one lie: they cannot be carried out only from above. Nothing can be done unless, when the time is ripe, the people directly concerned are motivated and capable of acting. For this reason, since the direct action of citizens is always *also* required, it is necessary for them to feel that what they do is on their own initiative (even though it is "kindly co-ordinated" by public entities). Similarly, the public entity must leave them the necessary decision-making and operational space. Ultimately, this means that it is the people directly concerned who must have the power to decide what to do and how to do it.

Having said this, however, we should add that the birth and diffusion of bottom-up initiatives like the ones described in these examples would never have happened without adequate governance, without the ability to build a city-scale enabling ecosystem and to acknowledge it as a participatory ecosystem. It is not easy for a public body to move in this way. Indeed, it is not only a matter of letting citizens take part in discussions; it also entails giving them part of the power to make decisions and implement them. This in turn calls for a radical change in governance and considerable political commitment.[15]

Therefore, the example of Milan has led us to confirm what we anticipated: by promoting and supporting social innovation, the enabling systems of collaborative cities offer topics and arenas for discussion on what to do and how to

---

[15] E. Manzini and E. Staszowski, *Public and Collaborative* (DESIS Network: Milan, 2013) (http://www.desisnetwork.org/wp-content/uploads/192017/04/DESIS_PUBLIColab-Book.pdf).

do it. Therefore, they lead active citizens to design projects collaboratively and set a new form of participatory democracy in motion, one that we shall call project-centered democracy.

Making things happen

The scenario of project-centered democracy. Let's imagine society as an interweaving mesh of networks of people intent on discussing and making decisions about what to do and doing (or trying to do) what they have decided. The environment in which this is happening may be more or less favorable, meaning that it may make it more or less probable that such conversations take place and that, focusing on the common interest, they become decisions and then collaborative actions. The environment in which all this can happen in the best way imaginable is democracy. More precisely, it is *project-centered democracy*, meaning a participatory enabling ecosystem in which everybody can develop their projects and achieve their results, in so far as they do not reduce the possibility of other people doing the same. On the other hand, since we cannot design and produce alone, it is also a democracy that is born out of collaboration and produces collaboration. In doing so, it fosters the regeneration of social commons.

All this resonates with what the German philosopher Hannah Arendt wrote sixty years ago. For her, democracy should be depicted as a complex mesh of conversations on themes of common interest.[16] She also said that these conversations may emerge in public space and turn into concrete actions; that this passage from conversation to action is possible when people collaborate; and, finally, that this collaboration occurs when the common interest is made visible and representable. For

---

[16] Hannah Arendt, *The Human Condition*, 2nd edn. (Chicago: University of Chicago Press, 1958).

Arendt, interest is never individual: it is always an inter-being, something that exists between different human beings and something that must be defined and recognized in its social nature.[17] Because of this, I would add, pursuing this kind of interest always calls for collaboration between people, and it is this collaboration that gives people the power to make things happen. This is a power that, writes Arendt, is not offered by others but is born from their capacity to recognize common interests and collaborate to transform them into results. With these thoughts, Arendt offers us a useful background and language for our topic in a moment when, more than half a century later, what she imagined is, at least in principle, becoming technically possible: imagine a society of people who are capable of focusing on common interests and transforming them into actions on the world.

In this scenario, project-centered democracy is therefore an environment that tends to give everybody the possibility of meeting and collaborating and, in so doing, to achieve objectives pursuing interests that are both individual and collective. In this definition, the coexistence of these two planes, one personal and the other collective, is the characterizing aspect. If the environment were only to provide favorable conditions for individual projects, it might appear to offer people greater freedom, but this would only occur within the limits of what the system in which they would be operating was able, and willing to, offer. On the other hand, as we have seen, an environment that provides favorable conditions for collaborative projects gives space to coalitions that have, or can assume, the power to carry out their decisions. In other words, they can themselves build the conditions by which to accomplish what they wish to achieve. This is why project-centered democracy is also an environment that facilitates the

---

[17] Virginia Tassinari, contribution posted on DESIS Philosophy Talk, *Regenerating Democracy. A Design Contribution*, Transit Conference, Rotterdam, September 14, 2017.

creation of the distributed systems in which, as we said at the start of this chapter, people can make their own decisions on questions that concern them.

Given these characteristics, project-centered democracy is a form of participatory democracy that supports, integrates, and, hopefully, collaborates to regenerate other forms of democracy. It enriches them with ideas and practices from the new civicism of those who operate to produce value for themselves and for the community they belong to. The issue that arises now is to understand better how all this can happen, or in other words, how the relationship between these different forms of democracy will take shape.

We shall start with the following, rather obvious, consideration: the projects made possible by project-based democracy are the result of the actions of groups of citizens who are particularly sensitive to the issue in question. They are active citizens who find the time, attention, and energy required to participate. On the other hand, just because they are so active, these people are often not representative of the majority. Indeed, very often, the most interesting and dynamic experiences of social innovation have been promoted by small groups of active citizens who, at the beginning, were not understood by others. Sometimes, they were even in clear contrast to the ways of thinking and acting that were prevalent at that time and in that place.

However, these experiences, or at least the more successful ones, show us how to overcome this problem: if the ideas thought up and put into practice by small groups of citizens are good, they gradually spread, become more consistent, and are finally democratically discussed and approved. The neighborhood gardens, urban vegetable gardens, and organic food projects are clear examples of how this has in fact happened: at the beginning these activities were proposed and carried out only by small, fringe groups of activists (sometimes even illegally). Then, as we know, they grew in number and at a certain point, as we have seen with reference to the collaborative cities, they have been acknowledged and regularized by the public administration, which means that they have also been formally approved by the organisms of representative democracy.

It follows that in the participatory, enabling ecosystem we are talking about, a virtuous circle may develop between groups of active citizens, who informally generate new ideas, and the organisms of representative democracy, which have the authority to approve and institutionalize them. Thus, they are democratically approved and regulated, becoming part of a more favorable ecosystem.

Infrastructure for project-centered democracy. How can we create the conditions that make the existence of project-centered democracy more probable? How can we bring the group actions of active citizens and the practices of representative democracy together so they support each other? To discuss this, we shall return to the SITRA report already mentioned. In its conclusions it says, "Effective democracy requires diverse social structures where engagement can take place ... Social infrastructure is as necessary as the traditional infrastructure of roads and bridges ... The possible role of public authority in creating this social infrastructure is a question for the world of politics."[18] How can this infrastructure be produced for project-centered democracy? The experience of mature social innovation, and especially that of collaborative cities, enables us to answer this question. As we have seen in the example given, the infrastructure of project-centered democracy effectively corresponds to that of its enabling ecosystem. This equivalence of the enabling ecosystem and the participatory ecosystem can be generalized, so from here, we can reflect on the nature and characteristics of this ecosystem when it also plays the role of democratic infrastructure.[19]

---

[18] Elina Kiiski Kataja, *From the Trials of Democracy towards the Future Participation*, SITRA Memorandum, March 21, 2017.
[19] S. L. Star, X. Bowker, "How to Infrastructure," in L. A. Lievrouw and S. L. Livingstone (eds.), *The Handbook of New Media* (London: SAGE, 2002), pp. 151–162; E. Bjorgvinsson, P. Ehn, and P. A. Hillgren, *Participatory Design and*

Infrastructure is characterized by its capacity to support a variety of projects. To play this role, it must include various elements. First of all it must include the rules of the democratic game (which make sure that every project respects the right of the other projects to exist with equal possibility of succeeding), the physical and virtual arenas (where people can meet and decide on their aims and how to achieve them), the online services and offline support (which make the codesigning and coproduction activities more accessible and effective), and the social commons (such as trust and shared values that, as we have already seen, are the precondition for all forms of collaboration).

As well as these elements, infrastructure is also characterized by the way in which it supports the project activities. This is never in fact neutral; it always entails a certain orientation. We can refer to this characteristic as *affordance*:[20] the capacity of an artifact to invite a certain mode of use and a way of being that does not force any particular behavior but which makes it more probable than others. In our case, the *affordance* we are talking about is the capability of an infrastructure to orientate the projects it supports, which means that it invites their designing coalitions to consider the knowledge and values that are embedded within itself, that is, within that particular

---

Democratizing Innovation. In proceedings of participatory design conference (New York, NY, USA, 2010), pp. 43–49; Carl Di Salvo, "Design, Democracy and Agonistic Pluralism," Georgia Institute of Technology (http://www. democracy-design.org/wp-content/uploads/2017/05/Design-Democracy-and-Agonistic-Pluralism.pdf).

[20] The term "affordance" originally emerged in connection with physical objects to refer to the way their actual shape and form were able to suggest to the user how to use them: from how a door opens to the way to pour from a teapot. Indeed, this may be as effective even when the user has never seen the item before and without instructions. The term has since been extended to physical and virtual environments, indicating what their configuration invites one to do. James Jerome Gibson, *The Ecological Approach to Visual Perception* (Boston: Houghton Mifflin, 1979); Donald A. Normann, *The Psychology of Everyday Things* (New York: Basic Books, 1988).

infrastructure (and which are also the knowledge and values considered important by the community that originally conceived and created it).

For example, a local administration may offer areas or urban spaces to citizens who are designing projects, indicating some general principles to be adopted (by the project proposers) and committing themselves—that is, the local administration itself—to supporting the project. The result of this way of acting, which in Italy is called *Regolamento di collaborazione tra cittadini e amministrazione*[21] (regulations for collaboration between the local administration and citizens), constitutes a clear example of a participatory enabling system and hence of democratic infrastructure. The affordance of this infrastructure is equally clear: by indicating the way in which the parties are to participate and giving general principles, it stimulates and supports the creativity and enterprise of the citizens, orientating them toward the production of urban commons. In other words, the value of active citizenship and the value of the commons are incorporated in the infrastructure and its way of working.

It seems to me that the theme of affordance in democratic infrastructure is of great practical and theoretical importance. It is also delicate, in that it is easily misunderstood: How do we reconcile the orientation given by the affordance of the infrastructure, with the fact that democracy is, by definition, the regime where autonomy and diversity of opinions are cultivated? To answer this question, we have to keep in mind that, as I wrote before, democracy is also a regime capable of

---

[21] In these regulations, a local administration draws up a list of areas in which coalitions of citizens, associations, social enterprises, and private businesses can propose ideas about what to do and how to do it. Gregorio Arena and Christian Iaione, *L'età della condivisione. La collaborazione tra cittadini e amministrazione per i beni comuni* (Carrocci Editore: Roma, 2015).

For the Bologna example, see "Regolamento di collaborazione tra cittadini e amministrazione per la cura e la rigenerazione dei beni comuni urbani" (http://www.comune.bologna.it/sites/default/files/documenti/REGOLAMENTO%20 BENI%20COMUNI.pdf).

learning. This means that it is capable of accumulating well-pondered experiences, filtering the best and embedding them within itself in the form of shared knowledge and values. This means that cultivating diversity does not coincide with an idea of neutrality at all levels. For example, the idea of democracy we refer to today is not neutral toward human rights, and its infrastructures should include affordances capable of inviting us not to act against them. The same should be true, in the case of project-centered democracy, for certain basic themes we have been talking about: collaboration, the interweave of relationships between people and the places they live in, and regeneration of the commons. In short, we can say that the role of affordance is to connect the operational level of infrastructure (enabling projects) with the cultural level (orientating projects).

Diffuse design capabilities. However, having an appropriate infrastructure is not enough to make project-centered democracy possible; it also requires a diffuse design capability spread among a sufficient number of people. So, to increase potential, it is also necessary to increase the number of active citizens and for each of them to improve their design capability. This calls for appropriate intervention. Although the ability to design is a human capacity potentially available to all, to fulfill this potential it needs to be cultivated (just like any other human capacities—see Chapter 2).

The by now long experience in the field of participatory design and codesign can help by making numerous support tools available for designing projects. These not only enable the achievement of shared results but also have the beneficial collateral effect of improving the design capabilities of everybody involved. These tools should be brought to a wider public, making them more accessible and easier to use and hopefully become part of the normal basic culture of citizens.[22] In addition, since every design activity is not only a

---

[22] This theme is developed by Daniela Selloni in her book *CoDesign for Public-Interest Services*. From what the author says, we can infer that the diffusion

question of tools but also of ideas, values, knowledge, critical sense, and creativity, it is necessary to develop some basic competence along these lines too. In other words, people also need cultural tools that enable them to recognize the current problems and opportunities and imagine possible futures (other than those normally proposed).[23] Therefore, as well as the operational tools of codesign, it is crucial that an appropriate design culture be diffused among the people involved.

By the term "design culture," I mean here a mixture of values and knowledge deriving from the accumulation of reflections on previous experiences, the existence of which enables us to feed the social conversation and produce new ideas and shared visions.[24] In this book, I have tried to bring out its various elements: ranging from the value of complexity to that of lightness in the building of new communities; from the dialogical sense to give to one's own life projects to the recognition of their possible political implications; from the value of social

---

of design capability, or more precisely, the ability to participate in codesign processes, should itself be seen as a public-interest service. Daniela Selloni, *CoDesign for Public-Interests Services* (Springer International Publishing, Cham, Switzerland 2017). See also Thomas Binder, Eva Brandt, Pelle Ehn, and Joachim Halse, "Democratic Design Experiments: Between Parliament and Laboratory," *CoDesign* 11, no. 3–4 (2015), 152–165. DOI: 10.1080/15710882.2015.1081248.

[23] There is a line of thinking that maintains, not unreasonably, that the tools of participation, and of participatory design in particular, may also become tools for building consensus toward dominant interests. This concern is certainly legitimate, but I believe that the risk of this happening does not lie in codesign as such, but rather in the reductive interpretation that leads us to concentrate on the tools and forget the contents.

Karl Palma and Otto von Busch, "Quasi-Quisling: Co-design and the Assembly of Collaborateurs," *CoDesign* 11, no. 3–4 (2015), 236–249; Otto von Busch and Karl Palmås, *Social Means Do Not Justify Corruptible Ends: A Realist Perspective on Social Innovation and Design* (She Ji: *The Journal of Design, Economics, and Innovation*, June 2017).

[24] E. Manzini and V. Tassinari, "Sustainable Qualities: Powerful Drivers of Social Change," in R. Crocker, S. Lehmann (eds.), *Motivating Change* (London: Earthscan, 2013); Ezio Manzini, "Design Culture, Dialogic Design," *Design Issues* 32, no.1 (Winter 2016), 52–59.

activism to that of transformative normality. All these themes lead on to the same design issue: that of collaboration and the capacity to reconnect people and places, and in so doing to produce relational value and social commons.

As discussed, some of these themes, and the indications for action deriving from them, can be incorporated in the democratic infrastructure as affordance. Others can become part of the personal baggage of the various social actors, orientating their actions. Altogether, combined in different ways, they can become part of a project. Thus, they can feed the democratic life of a society, raising the level of discussion.

Indeed, project-centered democracy, just as any other form of democracy, is not a zero-sum game, in which the various voices annul one another. Rather, it is a social learning process: a great laboratory in which multivoiced experimentation takes place on how to precede toward fairer and more sustainable ways of living. The idea that I have tried to add is that the more the design capability of the participants is cultivated, the more productive this collective reflection will be, and thus the more this capability will be enriched by a design culture fitted to the complexity of a world that, whether we want to or not, we have to face up to.[25]

---

[25] The discussion about how design culture can collaborate to regenerate democracy must find new arenas in which to develop. One of these may be Democracy Design Platform (DDP), a digital platform created by DESIS Network and by Design Policy Lab at the Politecnico di Milano (http://www. democracy-design.org).

DDP intends to collect together and give visibility to initiatives associated with the question of participatory democracy and particularly with what is referred to in this book as project-centered democracy. DDP was created in 2017 following the open letter, "Stand Up for Democracy," sent by Victor Margolin and myself to spur readers to take a stand against the growing attacks on democracy and to promote regenerating activities (http://www. democracy-design.org/open-letter-stand-up-democracy).

Afterword: Another Book. Design Experts and Diffuse Design Capability

1. In this book, people who make design choices, whether or not they are aware of doing so, are considered to be designers. So, in the fluid, turbulent world we are immersed in today, this means potentially everybody. The book proposes a scenario where, with adequate support, these designers of everyday life can contribute to changing the world. For this to happen, it is necessary for design coalitions to form that are capable of experimenting new paths and learning from experience. However, the fact that everybody in these coalitions is a designer does not mean that they are all designers in the same way. There are different actors within them, with equally diverse competence and capabilities. There are people directly concerned with the issue at hand, who know it well because they live it every day, and there are those who bring knowledge and experience regarding specific aspects. Among them, there are also experts in design, meaning those who, even in traditional language, are known as designers: people who are trained to focus, develop, and use the culture and tools of design.

I have hardly mentioned them and their role in this book. One book cannot talk about everything, and in this book, I have tried to focus on the question of diffuse design capability and its possibilities. Now, however, after four chapters in which I have been talking about diffuse design capability, it would be useful to say a word about expert design and the relationship between the two.

2. What is the role of design experts in the new design coalitions? What exactly is their contribution? Many authors, including myself, have answered questions that may look similar: What role do the experts play in codesign processes? What role do they play in promoting and supporting social innovation? Although they converge with the questions posed in this book, they do not really coincide with them.

To discuss the role of design experts in design coalitions, we need to go back to everything found when talking about codesign and design for social innovation. However, this must be extended to new territories, the exploration of which requires further questions to be answered: What is the role of design experts in an ecosystem that is both enabling and participatory? How do they operate in transformative reality, balancing accessibility and the production of relational values? How do they stimulate and support a diffuse design culture that is capable of acting in autonomy from dominant ideas? Then, more generally: What is the role of design experts in building a collective design intelligence, one that cultivates diversity and critical sense to catalyze the necessary positive resources required to take us out of the environmental, social, and cultural catastrophe we are falling into?

All these are urgent questions. But another book is required to answer them.

INDEX